POPULAR MECHANICS

HOME HOW-TO

OUTDOORS
AND GARDENS

ALBERT JACKSON AND DAVID DAY

Copyright © 1989 by The Hearst Corporation

This work has been extracted from *Popular Mechanics Home How-To*
published by Hearst Books.

This book was created exclusively for William Collins Sons & Co. Ltd. by
Jackson Day Jennings Ltd., trading as Inklink.

It is the policy of William Morrow and Company, Inc., and its imprints and
affiliates, recognizing the importance of preserving what has been written, to
print the books we publish on acid-free paper, and we exert our best efforts
to that end.

Library of Congress Cataloging-in-Publication Data

Popular mechanics home how-to: outdoors and gardens.
p.   cm.
ISBN 0-688-10404-5
1. Outdoor spaces & design – do-it-yourself manual
I. Popular mechanics magazine
SB473.P59 1991 II. Title: Outdoors and gardens
712'.6—dc20   90-25833
                                                         CIP

Printed in the United States of America

First Edition

1 2 3 4 5 6 7 8 9 10

CONTENTS

Cross-references

When additional information about a subject is discussed in more than one section of the book, the subject is marked in the text with the symbol (▷). and the cross-references to it are listed in the margin of the page. Those printed in bold type are directly related to the task at hand. Other references that will broaden your understanding of the subject are printed in lighter type.

PLANNING A GARDEN

Designing plantings and structures for a yard is not an exact science. Plants may not thrive even though you select the right soil conditions and check the amount of daylight, and shrubs and trees may never reach the maximum size specified for them in a catalogue. Nevertheless, advance planning will produce a more satisfactory result than a haphazard approach, which could involve expensive mistakes like laying a patio where it will be in shade for most of the day, building a boundary wall that is too high to meet with zoning board approval, or putting in a patio that drains poorly. It is these permanent features of a garden which you should concentrate on planning first, always, of course, considering how they will fit and function. No one wants to live in a concrete jungle.

Deciding on the approach

Before you even put pencil to paper, get a feel for the style of yard you would prefer and consider whether it will sit happily with the house and its immediate surroundings. Is it to be formal, laid out in straight lines or geometric patterns—a style which often marries successfully with modern architecture? Do you prefer the more relaxed style of a rambling cottage garden? Natural informality may not be as easy to achieve as you think, and it will certainly take several years to mature into the established garden you have in mind. Or, consider a blend of both, where every plant, stone and pool of water is carefully positioned. A Japanese-style garden bears all the hallmarks of a man-made landscape yet conveys a sense of natural harmony.

There is no shortage of material from which to draw inspiration—countless books and magazines are devoted to the design of gardens. Don't expect to find a total solution which fits your plot exactly—no two gardens are alike—but you may be able to adapt a particular approach or develop a small detail into a design for your own garden. Visiting other gardens is even better. Large country estates and city parks will have been designed on a much grander scale, but at least you will be able to see how a mature shrub should look, or gain a fresh idea on combining plants, stone and water in a rockery or water garden. Don't forget that your neighbors and friends may also have had to tackle problems identical to yours. If nothing else, you might learn by their mistakes!

1 Cottage-style garden
The informal character of abundant flowers planted between areas of natural-stone paving ideally complements traditional architecture.

2 Consider the details
Good design does not rely on having a large garden. A successful combination of natural forms can be just as rewarding on a small scale.

3 A natural-looking rock garden
Once plants become established, a rock garden should blend into a landscape without a hint of artificiality. The effect relies on the careful positioning of stones during construction.

4 A simple layout
Simplicity is often the best approach, but the proportions of the various elements must be carefully considered to avoid a boring result.

SURVEYING THE PLOT

Measuring the plot
Measure your plot of land accurately, including the diagonals, because what might appear to be square or rectangular may taper towards one end or do something equally unexpected.

Slopes and gradients
Make a note of how the ground slopes. An accurate survey is not necessary, but at least jot down the direction of the slope and plot the points where it begins and ends. You can get some idea of the difference in levels by using a long straightedge and a level. Place one end of the straightedge on the top of a bank, for instance, and measure the vertical distance from the other end to the foot of the slope.

Climatic conditions
Check the path of the sun and the direction of prevailing winds. Don't forget that the angle of the sun will be higher in summer and a screen of deciduous trees will be less of a windbreak when they drop their leaves.

Soil conditions
Make a note of soil conditions. You can easily adjust soil content by adding peat or fertilizers. A peat or clay soil is not very stable, however, and will affect the type of footings and foundation you may want to lay.

Existing features
Plot the position of features you want to retain in your plan, such as existing pathways, areas of lawn, established trees and so on.

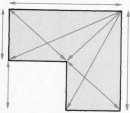

Measuring a plot
Note the overall dimensions, including the diagonals, to draw an accurate plan.

Gauging a slope
Use a straightedge and level to measure the height of a bank.

1△

◁2

3▷

4▽

1 Japanese-style garden
The overall effect should be one of tranquillity.

2 Using textures
Still water punctuated with rugged stones makes for a pleasing contrast of textures.

3 A sloping site
Some of the most dramatic gardens are a result of having to contend with a sloping site. Here, retaining walls are used to terrace a steep bank of colorful shrubs.

4 A formal garden
Use public parks or country estates as inspiration for planning a formal garden. These miniature hedges with selected plantings outline a geometric layout of pathways.

YARD PLANNING: BASIC CONSIDERATIONS

Having surveyed your plot, it is worth taking the time to plan all aspects of the design of your garden. Practical problems will need careful thought.

DRAWING A PLAN

Draw a plan of your garden on paper. It must be a properly scaled plan or you are sure to make some gross errors, but it need not be professionally perfect. Use graph paper to plot the dimensions, but do the actual drawing on tracing paper laid over the graph paper. This allows you to try out several different ideas and adapt your plan without having to redraw it every time.

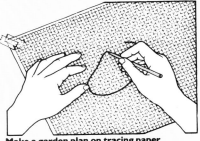
Make a garden plan on tracing paper

PLOTTING YOUR DESIGN

Planning on paper is only the first stage. Gardens are rarely seen from above, so it is essential to plot the design on the ground to check your dimensions and view the features from different angles. A pond or patio which looks enormous on paper can be pathetically small in reality. Other shortcomings, such as the way a tree will block the view from your proposed patio, become obvious once you lay out the plan full-size.

Plot individual features by driving pegs into the ground and stretching string lines between them. Scribe arcs on the ground with a rope tied to a peg, and mark the curved lines with stakes or a row of bricks. Use a garden hose to mark out less regular curves and ponds. If you can scrape areas clear of weeds, it will define the shapes still further.

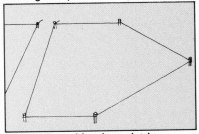
Mark out lines with stakes and string

PRACTICAL EXPERIMENTS

When you have marked out your design, check that it works with a few practical experiments. Will it be possible, for instance, for two people to pass each other on a footpath without stepping onto flowerbeds? Can you set down a wheelbarrow onto the path without one of its legs slipping into the pond?

Try placing some furniture on the area marked out for a patio to make sure you can sit comfortably and even serve a meal when visitors arrive. Most people build a patio alongside the house, but if you have to put it elsewhere to find a sunny spot, will it become a chore to walk back and forth for food?

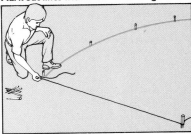
Use rope tied to a peg to scribe an arc

SITING PONDS

Site a pond to avoid overhanging trees and where it will catch at least a half-day's sunlight. Check that you can reach it with a hose for filling and that you can run electrical cables to power a pump or decorative lighting.

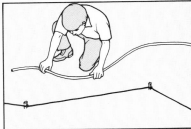
Try out irregular curves with a garden hose

COMMON-SENSE SAFETY

Don't make your garden an obstacle course. A narrow path alongside a pond, for instance, could be intimidating to an elderly relative. Low walls or planters near the edge of a raised patio could cause someone to trip.

DRIVEWAYS AND PARKING SPACES

Allow a minimum width of 10 feet for a driveway, making sure there is enough room to open the car doors if you park alongside a wall. Remember that vehicles larger than your own might need to use the drive or parking space—delivery trucks, for instance. When you drive in or out, will you be able to see? Try out the turning circle of your car in an empty parking lot.

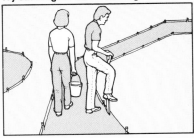
Make sure two people can pass on a path

CONSIDER THE NEIGHBORS

There may be legal restrictions on what you can erect in your garden (◁), but even if you have a free hand it is only wise to consult your neighbors if anything you plan might cause discomfort or inconvenience. A wall or even trees which are high enough to shade their favorite sun spot or block out the light to a window could be the source of argument for years to come.

TREE ROOTS AND FOUNDATIONS

As a permanent feature of your yard, you will probably want to plant at least one tree. You will need to think carefully about your choice of trees and their position—they could be potentially damaging to the structure of the house if planted too near.

GROWING IVY ON WALLS

There is a widely held misconception that a climbing ivy will damage any masonry wall. If stucco or the mortar between bricks or stonework is in a poor condition, then an exuberant ivy plant will undoubtedly weaken the structure as its aerial roots attempt to extract moisture from the masonry. The roots invade broken joints or cracks and on finding a source of nourishment for the main plant, they expand and burst the weak material, which accelerates deterioration by encouraging moisture penetration. If the ivy is allowed to grow unchecked, the weight of the plant can eventually topple a weakened wall.

However, with modern hard bricks and mortar, ivy can do no more than climb by the aid of training wires and its own suckerlike roots. So long as the structure is sound and moistureproof, there is some benefit from ivy clothing a wall in that its close-growing mat of leaves, mostly with their drip tips pointing downwards, acts as insulation and a watershed against the elements. Where ivy is permitted to flourish as a climber, it must be hard-pruned to prevent it from penetrating between roofing joints and vents and clogging gutters and downspouts.

Don't allow ivy to grow out of control

Cracks: subsidence and heaving

Minor cracks in siding, stucco and even brickwork are often the result of shrinkage as the structure dries out. These sorts of cracks are not serious and can be repaired during normal maintenance, but more serious structural cracks are due to movement of foundations. Trees planted too close to a building can add to the problem by removing moisture from the site, causing subsidence of the foundations as the supporting earth collapses. The felling of trees can be just as damaging. The surrounding soil, which had become stabilized over the years, swells as it takes up the moisture which had been removed previously by the tree root system. Upward movement of the ground, known as heave, distorts the foundations until cracks appear.

Siting trees

Growing tree roots search out moisture, and this can result in an expensive repair or replacement of the house drainage system. Large roots can fracture rigid pipework or penetrate joints until the drain becomes blocked.

Before you plant a tree close to a building, find out the likely spread of the mature root system. As a rough guide, make sure there is a distance of at least two-thirds the mature height of a tree between it and nearby buildings. If an existing tree is likely to cause a problem, ask your local building department for advice—the tree may be protected by a preservation order and you could be fined if you cut it down without permission. It may be possible to prune the branches and roots to lessen the likelihood of future damage.

SEE ALSO

Details for: ▷
Repairing cracks   23

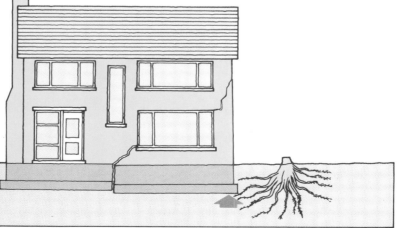

Subsidence
A mature tree planted close to a house can drain so much water from the ground that the earth collapses, causing the foundation to subside.

Heave
When a mature tree is felled, the earth can absorb more water, causing it to swell until it displaces the foundation of a building.

FENCES: CHOOSING

A fence is the most popular form of boundary marker or garden screen because of its advantages over other methods of dividing plots of land. A fence takes very little time to erect when compared with a wall or especially a hedge, which takes years to establish. Most fencing components are relatively lightweight and are therefore easy to transport and handle on site.

Economics and maintenance

In the short term a fence is cheaper than a wall built of masonry, although one can argue that the cost of maintenance and replacement over a very long period eventually cancels out the saving in cost. Wood does have a comparatively short life because it is susceptible to insect infestation and rot (◁) when exposed to the elements, but a fence will last for many years if it is treated regularly with a chemical preservative. In any case, if you are prepared to spend a little more money on plastic or concrete components, you can erect a virtually maintenance-free fence.

Choosing your fencing

When you measure even a small garden, you will be surprised by the overall length of fencing required to surround your property, so it is worth considering the available options carefully to make sure that you invest your money in the kind of fence that will be most suitable. Unless your priority is to keep neighborhood children or animals out of your garden, the amount of privacy afforded by a fence is likely to be your most important consideration. There are a number of privacy options, but you may have to compromise to some extent if you plan to erect a fence on a site exposed to strong prevailing winds. In that case you will need a fence which will provide a decent windbreak without offering such resistance that the posts will work loose within a couple of seasons due to constant buffeting by the wind.

Planning and planning permission

You can build any fence up to about 6 feet high without a zoning variance (◁) unless your boundary adjoins a highway, in which case permissible fence height may be limited. In addition, there may be local restrictions on fencing if the land surrounding your house has been designed as an open-plan area. Even so, many authorities will permit low boundary markers such as a ranch-style or post-and-chain fence.

At least discuss your plans with your neighbors, especially as you will require their permission to enter onto their properties, and it is always an advantage to be able to work from both sides when erecting a fence. Check the line of the boundaries to make certain that you do not encroach on neighbors' land. The fence posts should run along the boundary or on your side of the line. Before you dismantle an old fence, make sure it is yours to demolish. If a neighbor is unwilling to replace an unsightly fence, or even to allow you to replace it at your expense, there is nothing to stop you from erecting another fence alongside as long as it is on your property. It is an unwritten law that a good neighbor erects a fence with the post and rails facing his or her own property, but there are no legal restrictions which force you to do so.

Chain-link fencing

Trellis fencing

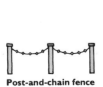

Post-and-chain fence

TYPES OF FENCING

CHAIN-LINK FENCING

Chain-link fencing is a utilitarian form of barrier constructed from wire netting stretched between fence posts. A true chain-link fence is made from strong galvanized or plastic-coated wire woven into a diamond-shape mesh, suspended from a heavy-gauge wire tensioned between the posts. A cheap fence can be made from soft wire netting or chicken wire. However, it is not very durable and will stretch out of shape if a large animal leans against it. Decorative wire fencing is available at many garden centers; it is designed primarily for low boundary markers or to support lightweight climbing plants. In fact, any chain-link fence will benefit from a screen of climbers or hedging plants.

TRELLIS FENCING

A concertina-fold trellis formed from thin softwood or cedar laths joined together is virtually useless as a fence in the true sense, relying exclusively on the posts and rails for its strength. But a similar fence made from split rustic poles nailed to heavy rails and posts forms a strong and attractive barrier. Both types of trellises are ideally suited as plant supports for climbers.

POST-AND-CHAIN FENCING

A post-and-chain fence is simply a decorative feature to keep people from wandering off a path or pavement onto a lawn or flowerbed. Lengths of painted metal or plastic chain are strung between short posts sunk into the ground.

TYPES OF FENCING

CLOSEBOARD FENCING

A closeboard fence is made by nailing overlapping bevel siding or "featherboard" strips to the horizontal rails. Featherboards are sawn planks which taper across their width from ⅝ inch at the thicker side down to about ⅛ inch. The boards are 4 to 6 inches wide, and the best quality are made from cedar. However, treated pine may also be used. Although it is expensive, closeboard fencing forms a strong and attractive screen. Being fixed vertically, the boards are difficult to climb from the outside—ideal for keeping children out!

Closeboard fencing

SEE ALSO

Details for: ▷

PREFABRICATED PANEL FENCING

Fences made from prefabricated panels nailed between wood posts are very common, perhaps because they are particularly easy to erect. Standard panels are 6 feet wide, and rise in 1-foot steps from approximately 2 feet to 6 feet in height. Most panels are made from interwoven or overlapping strips of pine or cedar sandwiched between a frame of 2 × 4s. The overlapping strip panels may be either sanded or rough-sawn. Some panels are pressure-treated to resist decay. Cedar may be left untreated to weather naturally.

A panel fence offers good value as a reasonably durable screen. But choose the lapped type for privacy. In the summer, interwoven strips will shrink to some extent, leaving gaps.

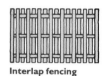

Panel fence

INTERLAP FENCING

An interlap fence is made by nailing square-edged boards to the horizontal rails, fixing them alternately on one side, then the other. Spacing is a matter of choice. For privacy, overlap the edges of the boards, or space them apart for a decorative effect.

This is the type of fence to choose for a windy site as it is substantial, yet the gaps between the boards allow the wind to pass through without exerting too much pressure. Because of its construction, an interlap fence is equally attractive from either side.

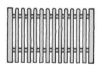

Interlap fencing

PICKET FENCING

The traditional, low picket fence is still popular as a barrier at the front of the house where a high fence is unnecessary. Narrow, vertical poles, with rounded or pointed tops, are spaced about 2 inches apart. As they are laborious to build by hand, most picket fences are sold as ready-made panels constructed from softwood or plastic to keep down the cost.

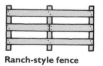

Picket fencing

RANCH-STYLE FENCING

Low-level fences made from simple, horizontal rails fixed to short, stout posts are the modern counterpart of picket fencing. Used extensively in today's housing developments, this ranch-style fencing is often painted, although clear-finished or stained wood is just as attractive and far more durable. Softwoods and some hardwoods are used for fencing, but plastic ranch-style fences are becoming increasingly popular for their clean, crisp appearance, since they do away with the chore of repainting for maintenance.

Ranch-style fence

CONCRETE FENCING

A cast concrete fence offers the security and permanence of a masonry wall and needs minimal maintenance. Interlocking, horizontal sections are built one upon the other up to the required height. Each screen is supported by grooves cast into the sides of specially designed concrete fence posts.

Concrete fencing

FENCE POSTS

Whatever type of fence you plan to erect on your property, its strength and durability rely on good-quality posts set solidly in the ground. Buy the best posts you can afford, and erect them carefully. It is worth taking longer over its construction to avoid having to dismantle and repair a poorly built fence in the future.

TYPES OF POSTS

In some cases, the nature of the fencing will determine the choice of post. Concrete fencing, for instance, must be supported by compatible concrete posts, but usually, you can choose the material and style of post which suits the appearance of the fence.

TIMBER POSTS

Most fences are supported by square-section wooden posts. Standard nominal sizes are 4 × 4 and 6 × 6 inches; 8 × 8 posts are also available. Most lumberyards supply pretreated softwood posts unless you ask specifically for hardwood.

CONCRETE POSTS

A variety of 4 × 4-inch reinforced-concrete posts exists to suit different styles of fence: drilled for chain-link, mortised for rails and recessed or grooved for panels. Special corner and end posts are notched to accommodate bracing struts for chain-link fencing.

METAL POSTS

Angle iron or plastic-coated steel posts are made to support chain link or plastic fences. Although angle iron posts are very sturdy, they do not make for a very attractive garden fence.

PLASTIC POSTS

PVC posts are supplied with plastic fencing, but most have to be reinforced internally by a wooden insert for fences over 2 feet 6 inches in height.

Preserving fence posts

Even when a wood post is pretreated to prevent rot, provide additional protection by soaking the base of each post in a bucket of chemical preservative for at least ten minutes, and longer if possible (◁).

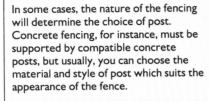

Capping fence posts
If you simply cut the end of a timber post square, the top of the post will rot relatively quickly. The solution is to cut a single or double bevel to shed the rainwater, or nail a wooden or galvanized metal cap over the end of the fence post.

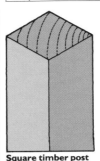

Square timber post

Drilled concrete post

Mortised concrete post

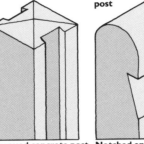

Grooved concrete post

Notched end post

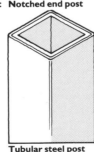

Angle iron post

Tubular steel post

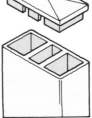

Capped plastic post

REMOVING OLD FENCE POSTS

Fixing posts in virgin soil is straightforward, but if you are replacing a fence you may want to put the new posts in the same positions as the old ones. Remove the topsoil from around each post to loosen the grip of the soil. If one is bedded firmly, or sunk into concrete, lever it out as shown below. Drive large nails in two opposite faces of the post, about 1 foot from the ground. Bind a length of rope around the post just below the nails, and tie the ends to the tip of a length of heavy lumber. Build a pile of bricks close to the post and use it as a fulcrum to lever the post out of the ground.

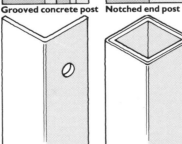

Levering a rotted fence post
Use a pile of bricks as a fulcrum to lift the post.

FIXING TO A WALL

If a fence runs up to the house, fix the first post to the wall with three expanding masonry bolts. Place a washer under each bolt head to stop the wood from being crushed. Check with a level that the post is vertical, driving shims between the post and wall to make slight adjustments.

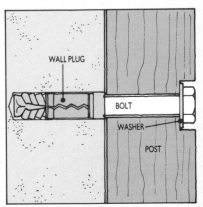

Bolting a post to a wall
If you are fitting a prefabricated panel against a wall-fixed post, counterbore the bolts so that the heads lie flush with the surface of the wood.

USING METAL SPIKES

Instead of anchoring fence posts in concrete, you can plug the base of each post into the square socket of a metal spike driven into firm ground. Use a 2-foot spike for fences up to 4 feet high, but use a 2-foot 6-inch spike for a 6-foot-high fence.

Place a scrap of hardwood post into the socket to protect the metal, then drive the spike partly into the ground with a sledgehammer. Hold a level against the socket to make certain the spike is plumb (1). Continue to hammer the spike into the ground until only the socket is visible. Insert the post and secure it by screwing through the side of the socket or by tightening clamping bolts (2), depending on the design of the spike you are using.

If you are erecting a panel fence, use the edge of a fixed panel to position the next spike (3).

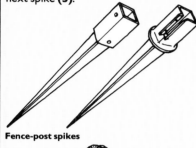

Fence-post spikes

1 Check with a level that spike is vertical

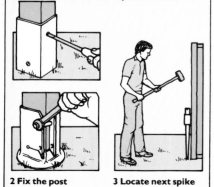

2 Fix the post   **3 Locate next spike**

ERECTING FENCE POSTS

The type of fence you choose to erect often dictates whether you erect all the posts first or one at a time along with the other components. When building a prefabricated panel fence, for instance, fix the posts in the ground as you erect the fence, but complete the run of posts before you install chain-link fencing.

Marking out

Drive a stake into the ground at each end of the fence run and stretch a line between. If possible, adjust the spacing of the posts to avoid obstructions such as large tree roots. If one or more posts have to be inserted across a paved patio, lift enough slabs to dig the necessary holes. You may have to break up a section of concrete beneath the slabs using a cold chisel and hammer.

Erecting the posts

Digging the hole

Bury one-quarter of each post to provide a firm foundation. For a 6-foot-high fence, dig a 2-foot hole to take an 8-foot post. You can rent a post hole auger to remove the central core of earth. Twist the tool to drive it into the ground (1) and pull it out after every 6 inches to remove the soil. When you have reached a sufficient depth, taper the sides of the hole slightly so that you can pack gravel and concrete around the post.

Anchoring the post

Ram a layer of gravel, broken bricks or small stones into the bottom of the hole to support the base of the post and provide drainage. Get someone to hold the post upright while you brace it with supports nailed to the post and to stakes driven into the ground (2). Use a level to check that it is vertical. (Use guy ropes to support a concrete post.)

Pack more coarse fill around the post, leaving a hole about 2 feet deep for filling with concrete. Mix some concrete to a firm consistency using the proportions 1 part cement: 2 parts sand: 3 parts aggregate ($\triangleright$). Use a trowel to drop concrete into the hole all around the post and tamp it down with the end of a 4 × 4 (3). Build the concrete just above the level of the soil and smooth it to slope away from the post (4). This will help shed water and prevent rot. Let the concrete harden for about a week before removing the struts. To support a panel fence temporarily, wedge struts against the posts.

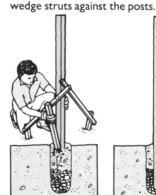

1 Dig the post hole   **2 Brace the post**   **3 Fill with concrete**   **4 Slope the concrete**

Supporting end posts

Chain-link fence posts must resist the tension of the straining wires ($\triangleright$). Brace each end post (and some intermediate posts ($\triangleright$) over a long run) with a strut made from a length of fence post. Shape the end of the strut to fit a notch cut into the post (1) and nail it in place. Order special posts and precast struts for concrete components.

Anchor the post in the ground in the normal way, but dig a 1½-foot-deep trench alongside for the strut. Wedge a brick under the end of the strut before tamping gravel around the post and strut. Fill the trench up to ground level with concrete (2).

Support a corner post with two struts set at right angles. Where a fence adjoins a masonry wall, fix as described in the box on the opposite page.

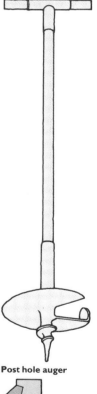

Post hole auger

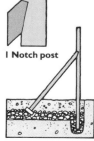

1 Notch post

2 Concreting end post

11

ERECTING A CHAIN-LINK FENCE

Set out a complete row of wood, steel, concrete or angle iron posts to support chain-link fencing, spacing them no more than 10 feet apart. Brace the end posts with struts (◁) to resist the pull of the straining wires. A long run of fencing will need a braced intermediate post every 225 feet or so.

Using wooden posts

Support the chain-link fencing on straining wires (see right). As it is impossible to tension this heavy-gauge wire by hand, use large straining bolts to stretch it between the posts. Mark the height of each wire on the posts—one to coincide with the top of the fencing, one about 6 inches from the ground, and the third midway between. Drill ⅜-inch-diameter holes right through the posts, insert a bolt into each hole and fit a washer and nut, leaving enough thread to provide about 2 inches of movement once you begin to apply tension to the wire (**1**).

Pass the end of the wire through the eye of a bolt and twist it around itself with pliers (**2**). Stretch the wire along the run of fencing, stapling it to each post and strut, but leaving enough slack for the wire to move when tensioned (**3**). Cut the wire to length and twist it through the bolt at the other end of the fence. Tension the wire from both ends by turning the nuts with a wrench (**4**).

Standard straining bolts provide enough tension for the average garden fence, but over a long run (200 feet or more), use a turnbuckle for each wire, applying tension with a metal bar (see left).

Using concrete posts

Fix straining wires to concrete posts using a special bolt and cleat (see right). Bolt a stretcher bar to the cleats when putting on the wire netting.

Tie the straining wire to intermediate posts with a length of galvanized wire passed through the predrilled hole.

Using angle iron posts

Winding brackets are supplied with angle iron fence posts to attach stretcher bars and to apply tension to the straining wires (see right). As you pass the straining wire from end to end, pass it through the predrilled hole in every intermediate post.

Using a turnbuckle
Apply tension by turning the turnbuckle with a metal bar.

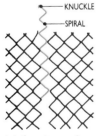

Joining wire mesh
Chain-link fencing is supplied in standard lengths. To join one roll to another, unfold the knuckles at each end of the first wire spiral, then turn the spiral counterclockwise to withdraw it from the mesh. Connect the two rolls by rethreading the loose spiral in a clockwise direction through each link of the mesh. Bend over the knuckle at the top and bottom.

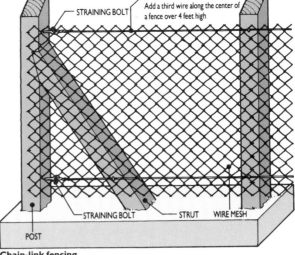

STRAINING WIRE
Add a third wire along the center of a fence over 4 feet high

STRAINING BOLT

STRAINING WIRE

STRAINING BOLT — STRUT — WIRE MESH

POST

Chain-link fencing

Attaching the mesh
Staple each end link to the post. Unroll the mesh and pull it taut. Tie it to straining wires every foot or so with galvanized wire. Fix to post at other end.

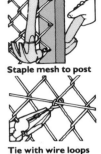

Staple mesh to post

Tie with wire loops

1 Insert a straining bolt in the end post

2 Attach a straining wire to the bolt

3 Staple the wire to the post and strut

4 Tension the bolt at far end of fence

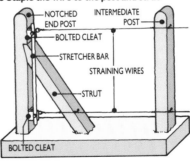

NOTCHED END POST — INTERMEDIATE POST
BOLTED CLEAT
STRETCHER BAR
STRAINING WIRES
STRUT
BOLTED CLEAT

Concrete fence posts

Cleat and stretcher bar **Tie wire to post**

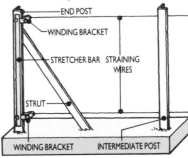

END POST
WINDING BRACKET
STRETCHER BAR STRAINING WIRES
STRUT
WINDING BRACKET INTERMEDIATE POST

Angle iron posts

Winding bracket **Pass wire through post**

ERECTING A CLOSEBOARD FENCE

The bevel siding panels used for this type of fence are nailed to triangular-section rails known as arris rails. The arris rails are mortised into the fence posts. Concrete posts—and some that are made of wood —are supplied ready-mortised, but if you buy standard timber posts you will have to cut the mortises, a job you may not want to do. The unprotected end grain of the panels is liable to rot, especially if they are in contact with the ground. So fix horizontal 1 × 6 gravel boards at the foot of the fence, and nail wooden capping strips across the tops of the bevel siding. Space the fence posts no more than 10 feet apart.

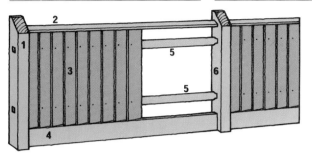

Closeboard fencing
1 End post
2 Capping strip
3 Featherboards
4 Gravel board
5 Arris rail
6 Intermediate post

REPAIRING A DAMAGED ARRIS RAIL

The arris rails take most of the strain when a closeboard fence is buffeted by high winds. Not surprisingly, they eventually crack across the middle or break where the tenon enters the mortise. You can buy galvanized metal brackets for repairing broken arris rails.

If you wish, you can use end brackets to construct a new fence instead of cutting mortises for the rails. However, it will not be as strong as a fence built with mortise-and-tenon joints.

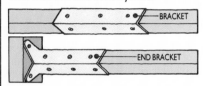

Erecting the framework

If you are using plain wooden posts, mark and cut mortises for the arris rails about 6 inches above and below the ends of the fixed paneling. For fencing over 4 feet high, cut mortises for a third rail midway between the others. Position the mortises about 1 inch from the front face of each post (the paneled side of the fence).

As you erect the fence, cut the rails to length and shape a tenon on each end with a coarse rasp or Surform file (**1**). Paint preservative onto the shaped ends and into the mortises before you assemble the rails.

Erect the first fence post and pack gravel around its base (▷). Get someone to hold the post steady while you fit the arris rails and erect the next post, tapping it onto the ends of the rails with a mallet (**2**). Check that the rails are horizontal and the posts are vertical before packing fill around the second post. Construct the entire run of posts and rails in the same way. If you cannot maneuver the last post onto tenoned rails, cut the rails square and fix them to the post with metal brackets (see box right).

Check the whole fencing run once more to ensure that the arris rails are bedded firmly in their mortises and that the framework is true. Then secure each rail by driving a nail through the post into the tenon (**3**). Or drill a hole through the post and tenon and insert a wooden dowel. Pack concrete around each post (▷). Allow it to cure.

Fitting the boards

Gravel boards
Some concrete posts are mortised to take gravel boards. In this case they must be fitted with the arris rails. To fit gravel boards to wooden posts, toenail treated wooden cleats at the foot of each post, then nail the gravel boards to the cleats (**4**).

If a concrete post is not mortised for gravel boards, set wooden cleats into the concrete filling at the base of the post, and screw the board to the cleat when the concrete is set.

Featherboards
Cut the featherboards to length and treat the end grain. Stand the first board on the gravel board with its thick edge against the post. Nail the board to the arris rails with galvanized nails positioned ¾ inch from the thick edge. Place the next board in position, overlapping the thin edge of the fixed board by ½ inch. Check that it is vertical, then nail it in the same way. Don't drive a nail through both boards or they will not be able to move when they shrink. To space the other boards equally, make a spacer block from a scrap of wood (**5**). Place the last board to fit against the next post and fix it, this time with two nails per rail (**6**).

When the fence is completed, nail capping strips across the tops of the featherboards, cut the posts to length and cap them (▷).

1 Shape the arris rails to fit mortises

2 Tap post onto rails

3 Nail rails in place

CLEAT

4 Nail gravel boards to the cleats

5 Position panels with a spacer block

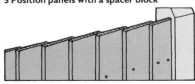

6 Fix last board with two nails

Capping the fence
Nail a wooden capping strip to the ends of the featherboards to shed rainwater.

ERECTING A PANEL FENCE

To prevent a prefabricated panel from rotting, either fit gravel boards as for a closeboard fence or leave a gap at the bottom by supporting a panel temporarily on two bricks while you nail it to the fence posts.

Using timber posts

Pack the first post into its hole with gravel (◁), then get someone to hold a panel against the post while you toenail through its framework into the post (**1**). If you can work from both sides, drive three nails from each side of the fence. If the frame starts to split, blunt the nails by tapping their points with a hammer. Alternatively, use metal angle brackets to secure the panels (**2**). Construct the entire fence erecting panels and posts alternately.

Nail capping strips across the panels if they have not been fitted by the manufacturer. Finally, cut each post to length and cap it (◁).

Wedge struts made from scrap lumber against each post to keep it vertical, then top up the holes with concrete (◁). If you are unable to work from both sides, you will have to fill each hole as you build the fence.

Using concrete posts

Panels are supported by grooved concrete posts without additional fasteners (**3**). Recessed posts are supplied with metal brackets for fastening the panels with screws (**4**).

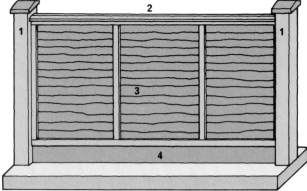

Panel fence
1 Fence posts
2 Capping strip
3 Prefabricated panel
4 Gravel board

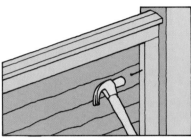

1 Nail the panel through its framework

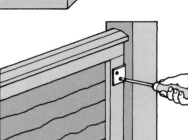

2 Or use angle brackets to fix panel to posts

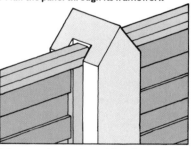

3 A grooved concrete post for a fence panel

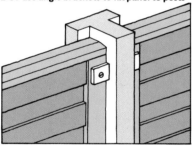

4 A recessed concrete post with bracket

Building a panel fence
Posts and panels are erected alternately. Dig a hole for the post (**1**) and hold it upright with gravel fill (◁). Support a panel on bricks (**2**) and have a helper push it against the post (**3**) while you nail it (**4**). Fit gravel boards (**5**), capping strips (**6**) and cap the posts (**7**). Fill the holes with concrete (**8**) and allow it to set.

ERECTING A POST-AND-RAIL FENCE

A simple ranch-style fence is no more than a series of horizontal rails fixed to short posts set into concrete in the normal way (▷). A picket fence is made in a similar way, but with vertical poles fixed to the rails.

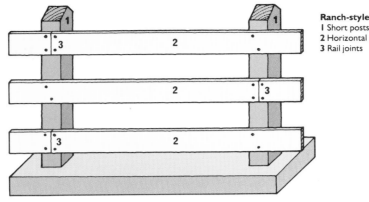

Ranch-style fence
1 Short posts
2 Horizontal rails
3 Rail joints

Fixed horizontal rails

You can simply screw the rails directly to the posts (1), but the fence will last longer if you cut a shallow notch in the posts to locate each rail before you join it permanently (2).

Join two rails by butting them over a post (3). Arrange to stagger these joints so that you don't end up with all the rails butted on the same post (4).

Fastening picket panels

When you construct a picket fence from ready-made panels, buy or make metal brackets for fixing two panels to a single post.

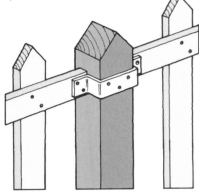

Use a metal bracket to fix picket-fence panels

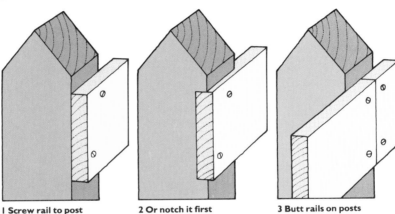

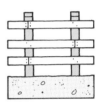

1 Screw rail to post **2 Or notch it first** **3 Butt rails on posts** **4 Stagger rail joints**

Supporting a rotted post

A buried timber post will quite often rot below ground level, leaving a perfectly sound section above. To save buying a whole new post, brace the upper section with a concrete spur.

Erecting a spur
Dig the soil from around the post and remove the rotted stump. Insert the spur and pack gravel around it (1), then fill with concrete (2). Drill pilot holes for coach screws—wood screws with hexagonal heads (3). Insert the screws with a wrench to draw the post tightly against the spur.

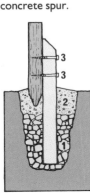

ERECTING FENCES ON SLOPING GROUND

Crossways slope
If a slope runs across the garden, so that your neighbor's garden is higher than yours, build brick retaining walls between the posts or set paving stones in concrete to hold back the soil.

Downhill slope
The posts must be set vertically even when you erect a fence on a sloping site. Chain-link fencing or ranch-style rails can follow the slope of the land if you wish, but fence panels should be stepped and the triangular gaps beneath filled with gravel boards or retaining walls.

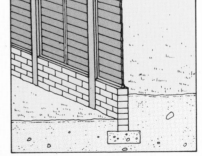

A retaining wall for a crossways slope

● **Building plastic fences**
The basic construction of a plastic ranch-style fence is similar to one built from wood. But follow the manufacturer's instructions concerning the method for joining rails to posts.

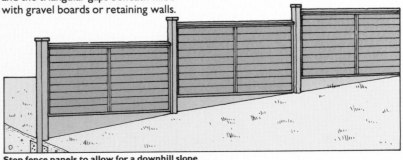

Step fence panels to allow for a downhill slope

15

GATES: CHOOSING

There are several points to consider when choosing a gate, not the least being the cost. All gates are relatively expensive, but don't buy one merely because it is cheaper than another. A garden gate must be constructed sturdily if it is to be reasonably durable, and, perhaps even more important, it must be mounted on strong posts.

Choose a style of gate which matches the fence or complements the wall from which it is hung, with due consideration for the character of the house and its surroundings. As a guide, aim for simplicity rather than the elaborate.

Side gates

Entrance gates

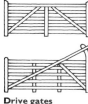

Drive gates

GATES FOR DIFFERENT LOCATIONS

When you browse through suppliers' catalogues, you will find gates grouped according to their intended location, because it is where it is to be sited that has most influence on the design of a gate and dictates its function.

SIDE GATES

A side gate is designed to protect a pathway next to a house from intruders. Side gates are invariably 6 feet 6 inches high and usually made from heavy lumber or metal. As a result, these gates are heavy and therefore braced with strong diagonal members to keep them rigid. With security in mind, choose a closeboard or tongue-and-groove gate—vertical boards are difficult to climb. When you hang a side gate, fit strong bolts top and bottom.

ENTRANCE GATES

An entrance gate is designed as much for its appearance as its function, but because it is in constant use, make sure it is properly braced with a diagonal strut running from the top of the latch stile down to the bottom of the hanging or hinge stile. If you hang a gate with the strut running the other way, the bracing will have no effect whatsoever.

Common fence structures are reflected in the style of entrance gates. Picket, closeboard and ranch-style gates are available, as is a simple and attractive frame and panel gate. With the latter style of gate, the solid wood or exterior-grade plywood panels keep the frame rigid. If the tops of both stiles are cut at an angle they will shed rainwater, reducing the likelihood of rot—a small but important feature to note when buying or designing a wooden gate.

Decorative iron gates are often used for entrances, but make sure the style is not too ostentatious for the building or its location. A very elaborate gate might look ridiculous in the entrance of a simple modern house or a traditional country cottage.

DRIVE GATES

First decide whether hanging a gate across a drive to a garage is such a good idea. Parking the car in a busy road in order to open the gate can be a difficult maneuver unless you have enough room to set the gate back from the entrance to leave enough space to pull the car off the road even when the gate is closed. Gates invariably open into the property, so make certain there is enough ground clearance for a wide gate if the drive slopes up towards a garage. Or hang two smaller gates to meet in the center. If you decide on a wide gate, choose a traditional five-bar gate for both strength and appearance.

GATE POSTS AND PIERS

Gate posts and masonry piers have to take a great deal of strain, so they must be strong in themselves and anchored securely in the ground.

Choose hardwood posts whenever possible, and select the section according to the weight of the gate. 4 × 4 posts are adequate for entrance gates but use larger posts for higher gates. For a wide gate across a drive, choose 6 × 6 or 8 × 8 posts.

Concrete posts are a possibility but unless you find a post predrilled to accept hinges and catch, you will have to screw them to a strip of lumber bolted to the post, so the fittings will not be securely fastened.

Square or tubular metal posts are available with hinge pins, gate-stop and catch welded in place. Like metal gates they must be protected from rust with paint, unless they have been coated with plastic at the factory.

A pair of masonry piers is another possibility. Each pier should be a minimum of 14 inches square and built on a firm concrete footing (◁). For large, heavy gates, the hinge pier at least must be very sturdy. It should be reinforced with a metal rod buried in the footing and running centrally through the pier.

HARDWARE FOR GATES

Rather specialized hardware has been developed to allow for the considerable strain on its hinges and catch imposed by a garden gate.

HINGES

Strap hinges
Side gates and most wooden entrance gates are hung on strap hinges, or T-hinges. Screw the long flap horizontally to the gate rails and the vertical flap to the face of the post. Heavier gates need a stronger version which is bolted through the top rail.

Wide drive gates need a double strap hinge with a long flap bolted on each side of the top rail. These heavy-duty hinges are supported by bolts which pass through the gate post.

Hinge pins
Metal collars, welded to the hinge side of metal gates, drop over hinge pins attached to gate posts in a variety of ways: screwed to wooden posts; bolted through concrete; built into the mortar joints of masonry piers; welded to metal posts. The gate can be lifted off its hinges at any time, unless you reverse the top pin or drill a hole and fit a split pin and washer.

LATCHES

Automatic latches
Simple wooden gates are fitted with a latch that operates automatically as the gate is closed. Screw the latch bar to the latch stile of the gate and use it to position the latch on the post.

Thumb latches
Cut a slot through a closeboard side gate for the latch lifter of a thumb or Suffolk latch. Pass the lifter bar through the slot and screw the handle to the front of the gate. Screw the latch bar to the inner face so that the lifter releases the bar from the catch plate.

Ring latches
A ring latch works in a similar way to a thumb latch but is operated from inside only, by twisting the ring handle to lift the latch bar.

Chelsea catches
Bolt a Chelsea catch through a drive gate. The latch pivots on the bolt to drop into a slot in the catch plate screwed to the post.

Loop-over catches
When two wide gates are used in a drive entrance, one gate is fastened with a drop bolt located in a socket set in concrete. A simple U-shaped metal bar, bolted through the latch stile of the other gate, drops over the stile of the fixed gate.

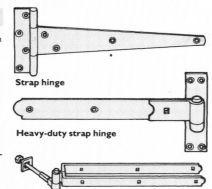
Strap hinge

Heavy-duty strap hinge

Double strap hinge

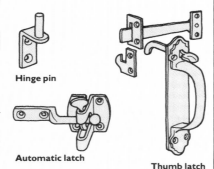
Hinge pin

Automatic latch

Thumb latch

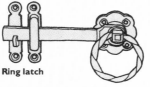
Ring latch

Chelsea catch

Loop-over catch

Materials for gates

Many wooden gates are made from softwood simply for economy, but a wood such as cedar or oak is a better investment. Most so-called wrought-iron gates are made from mild steel bar which must be primed and painted ($\triangleright$) if they are to last.

Hang a heavy drive gate on a stout post

GATE POSTS

Gate posts are set in concrete like ordinary fence posts but the post holes are linked by a concrete bridge to provide extra support.

Side and entrance gate posts

Lay the gate on the ground with a post on each side. Check that the posts are parallel and the required distance apart to accommodate hinges and catch. Nail two horizontal braces from post to post and another diagonally to keep the posts in line while you erect them (1).

Dig a 1-foot-wide trench across the entrance and long enough to accept both posts. It need be no deeper than 2 feet at the center, but dig an adequate post hole at each end—about 2 feet deep for a low entrance gate, 3 feet deep for a taller gate. Set the braced gate posts in the holes with gravel and concrete as for fence posts ($\triangleright$), using temporary braces to hold them upright until the concrete sets (2). Fill the trench with concrete at the same time and either level it flush with the pathway or allow for the thickness of paving slabs or blocks ($\triangleright$).

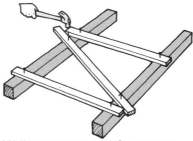
1 Nail temporary struts to the gate posts

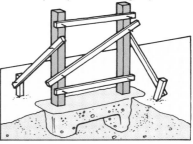
2 Support the posts until the concrete sets

Drive gate posts

Hang wide farm-style gates on posts set in 3-foot-deep holes (3). Erect the latch post in concrete like any fence post, but bolt a heavy piece of lumber across the base of the hinge post before anchoring it in concrete.

SEE ALSO

Details for:	$\triangleright$
Erecting posts	11
Paving slabs	48
Preservatives	70

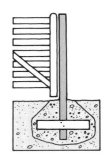
3 Drive gate post
Bolt a wood "deadman" to the post to help support the weight of the gate.

MASONRY: BUILDING WALLS

Whatever structure you build with masonry, the basic techniques for laying brick, stone or concrete block remain the same. On the other hand, it must be recognized that it is wise to hire a professional builder when the structure is complicated, extensive or must withstand considerable loads or stress.

A stone-built retaining wall

A boundary wall of yellow brick

Facing blocks make attractive dividing walls

A decorative pierced-block screen

Amateur bricklaying

It is difficult to suggest when a particular job is beyond the level of skill or confidence of an amateur bricklayer, clearly differing from individual to individual. It would be foolhardy for anyone to attempt to build a two-story house, for instance, unless they had had a lot of experience and, possibly, professional training, but building even a high boundary wall, which in terms of pure technique is simple, would be an arduous task if it were very long or had to allow for changes in gradient. The simple answer is to begin with low retaining or dividing walls and screens until you have mastered the skills of laying bricks and blocks solidly upon one another, and the ability to build a wall both straight and vertical without danger of possible collapse.

WALLS FOR DIFFERENT LOCATIONS

RETAINING WALLS

Raised planting beds are made with low retaining walls, but a true retaining wall is designed to hold back a bank of earth, usually to terrace a sloping site. As long as it is not too high, a retaining wall is easy to build, although, strictly speaking, it should slope back into the bank to resist the weight of the earth. Also, you must allow for drainage, to reduce the water pressure behind the wall. Retaining walls are built with bricks, concrete blocks or stone, sometimes dry-laid with earth packed into the crevices for planting—it is a matter of personal choice.

BOUNDARY WALLS

A brick or stone wall surrounding your property provides security and privacy while forming an attractive background to trees and shrubs. New, crisp brickwork complements a formal garden or modern setting, while second-hand materials or undressed stone blend with an old, established garden. If you cannort match exactly the color of existing masonry, encourage the growth of lichen with a wash of liquid fertilizer, or disguise the junction with a well-chosen climber. You may need local authority approval if you want to build a wall higher than 3 feet that will adjoin a road or public sidewalk (◁).

DIVIDING WALLS

Many gardeners divide a plot of land with walls to form a visual break between patio and lawn, to define the edges of pathways, or simply to add interest to an otherwise featureless site. Dividing walls are often merely low walls, perhaps only a foot or two in height. They make perfect structures upon which to practice basic techniques.

Use simple concrete block or brick walls to divide interior spaces—for a workshop or hobbies room.

SCREEN WALLS

Screens are also dividing walls, but they provide a degree of privacy without completely masking the garden beyond. Screens are built with decorative pierced blocks, often with solid block or brick bases and concrete piers.

STRUCTURAL WALLS

Walls of even a small building have to support the weight of a roof and, depending on the complexity of the structure, will have to incorporate door and window frames. In most cases, a moisture resistance will have to be built into the walls to control dampness, and some walls are constructed with a cavity between two leaves of masonry to provide insulation and weatherproofing. A brick foundation for a sun space is no more difficult to build than a simple garden wall, but make certain you are familiar with building methods before you attempt to build a garage or similar outbuilding.

CHOOSING BRICKS

More than 10,000 different types of bricks are produced in this country and throughout the world. Generally, your choice will be limited to bricks manufactured in your local area, since long-distance hauling of these heavy materials is prohibitively expensive. When creating brick designs and purchasing brick, it's important to understand the basic classifications as they relate to size, appearance and weathering characteristics.

The variety of brick

Face brick
Face bricks are suitable for any type of exposed brickwork. They are water- and frost-resistant. Being visible, face bricks are made as much for their appearance as their structural qualities and, as such, are available in the widest range of colors and textures. Face bricks are graded carefully to meet standards of strength, water absorption and uniformity of shape.

Building brick
Building bricks are cheap general-purpose bricks used primarily for interior brickwork which is to be plastered, or stuccoed if used externally. They are not color-matched carefully but the mottled effect of a wall built with building bricks is attractive.

Although they could become damaged or cracked by frost if used on an exposed site, building bricks can be used for garden walls.

Fire brick
Fire bricks are pale yellow in color and made from specially chosen clays and carefully fired. They're designed and used to line fireplaces, kilns and barbecues and must be laid with heat-resistant mortar.

Weathering classifications of brick

Building brick is manufactured in three grades that differentiate weathering characteristics and indicate the conditions a particular kind of brick is best suited for. For any particular project, check which kind of brick is required by the building department regulations in your area.

Type SW (severe weathering) bricks are best suited for outdoor projects in areas prone to prolonged periods of freezing. Always choose Type SW brick for patios and driveways. While there is a separate classification of bricks known as "paving bricks," these are meant for public, high-traffic areas and are not required for residential projects.

Type MW (moderate weathering) bricks can be used outdoors in areas where there is little or no frost. In most cases, Type MW bricks can be used for constructing garden walls, even in cold regions.

Type NW (no weathering) bricks are meant only for indoor use, but they can be used for outdoor structures where they'll be protected from the ravages of rain and snow.

Types of brick

Solid bricks
The majority of bricks are solid throughout, either flat on all surfaces or with a depression known as a "frog" on one face. When filled with mortar, the frog keys the bricks.

Cored or perforated bricks
Cored bricks are made with holes running through them, providing the same function as the frog. A wall made with cored bricks must be finished with a coping of solid bricks.

Special shapes
Specially shaped bricks are made for decorative brickwork. Master bricklayers use the full range to build arches, chamfered or rounded corners and curvilinear walls. A number of shaped bricks are made for coping garden walls.

BUYING BRICKS

Ordering bricks
Bricks are normally sold by the thousand, but builders' supply yards are usually willing to sell them in smaller quantities. It is cheaper to order them direct from the manufacturer, but only if you buy a sufficient load to make the delivery charge economical.

Estimating quantities
The size of a standard brick is $2\frac{1}{4} \times 3\frac{3}{4} \times 8$ inches, but because dimensions may vary by a fraction of an inch, even within the same batch of bricks, manufacturers normally specify a nominal size which includes an additional $\frac{1}{4}$ to $\frac{1}{2}$ inch to each dimension to allow for the mortar joint. To calculate how many bricks you need, allow about 48 bricks for every square yard of single-skin wall. Add a 5 percent allowance for cutting and breakage.

Storing bricks
When bricks are delivered, have them unloaded as near as possible to the building site, and stack them carefully on a flat, dry base. Cover the stack with polyethylene sheet or a tarpaulin until you are ready to use them, to prevent their becoming saturated with rain. This could cause staining and an increased risk of frost damage to the mortar and the bricks themselves.

The actual size of standard bricks

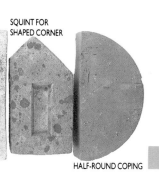

Types of brick

DOUBLE-CANT COPING

STANDARD BRICK WITH FROG

SQUINT FOR SHAPED CORNER

STANDARD CORED BRICK   BULLNOSE

HALF-ROUND COPING

THE COLOR AND TEXTURE OF BRICKS

The popularity of brick as a building material stems largely from its range of subtle colors and textures, which actually improve with weathering. Unfortunately, weathered brick can be difficult to match by using a manufacturer's catalogue. If you have spare bricks, take one to the supplier to compare with new bricks, or borrow samples from the supplier's stock to match when you get home.

Color

The color of bricks is determined by the type of clay used in their manufacture, although it is modified by the addition of certain minerals and the temperature of the firing. Large manufacturers supply a complete range of colors from black or purple to white, plus reds, browns and yellows. There are also brindled bricks—multicolored or mottled—especially useful for blending with existing masonry.

Texture

Texture is as important to the appearance of a brick wall as color. Simple rough or smooth textures are created by the choice of materials. Others are imposed upon the clay by scratching, rolling, brushing and so on. A brick may be textured all over or on the sides and ends only.

Brick colors and textures
A small selection from the extremely wide range of colors and textures.
1 Smooth blended
2 Handmade
3 Sand-faced yellow
4 Smooth blue engineering
5 Sand-faced gray
6 Smooth red stock
7 Wire-cut brindle
8 Textured multibuff
9 Second London stock
10 Wire-cut blue
11 Red common
12 Coarse fletton
13 Molded fletton
14 Dragwire multired

Pattern formed by projecting headers

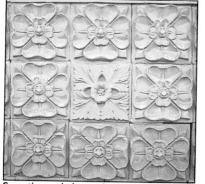

Decorative combination of colored bricks

Look out for second-hand molded bricks

Sometimes whole panels are available

Weathered antique bricks are attractive

CHOOSING CONCRETE BLOCKS

Cast concrete building blocks are not as standardized as clay bricks, but to describe them using the same specifications—variety, quality and type—makes for a useful comparison when choosing which to use.

Variety of block

Structural blocks
Simple rectangular blocks, cement gray or white in color, are used as the structural core of a wall which will be stuccoed or plastered. Consequently, they are often made with a zigzag key on the surface to encourage the finish to adhere. Since they are not intended as visible masonry, they have no aesthetic qualities whatsoever. A wall can be constructed quickly with blocks because they are considerably larger than standard bricks, and the wall will be relatively cheap.

Facing blocks
These are blocks with one decorative face and end for walls which are to be left exposed. They are often made to resemble natural stone by including crushed stone aggregate. There is a sufficient range of colors to blend with the local stone in most areas of the country. Facing blocks are used for the external skin of cavity walls, backed by the cheaper structural blocks. They are also used for ornamental garden walls for which matching coping slabs are available as a finishing touch.

Screen blocks
Screen blocks are pierced decorative building units for constructing a lightweight masonry trellis or screen. They are not bonded like brickwork or structural blocks and therefore require supporting piers made from matching pilaster blocks with locating channels to take the pierced blocks. Coping slabs finish the top of the screen and piers.

Quality of block

Load-bearing blocks
Structural blocks are used to construct the load-bearing walls of a building. Those made with lightweight aggregate are easier to handle, but when the loads are excessive, use stronger blocks made from dense concrete.

Nonload-bearing blocks
Nonload-bearing blocks are used to build internal, dividing partitions. They are either lightweight-aggregate blocks or low-density foamed-concrete blocks which are easy to cut to shape or chase for electrical wiring. Foamed blocks are also made in a load-bearing quality.

Decorative blocks
Pierced screen blocks should not be used in the construction of load-bearing walls. However, they are capable of supporting a lightweight structure such as a wood and plastic carport roof.

Insulating blocks
Foamed blocks are often used for constructing the inner leaf of a cavity wall. They have good insulating properties and meet minimum building code standards without the need for secondary insulation. Use ultralight foamed blocks when improved insulation is required.

Type of block

Solid blocks
Solid blocks are constructed two ways—with lightweight aggregate or foamed concrete.

Cored blocks
To reduce their weight, large dense-concrete blocks are virtually hollow with supporting ribs between the outer skins. Stretcher blocks are used for the main part of the wall, while corner blocks are used when the end of a wall is exposed. Solid-top blocks, partly hollowed out on the underside, are used to support joists.

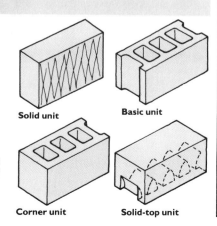

Solid unit

Basic unit

Corner unit

Solid-top unit

BUYING CONCRETE BLOCKS

Estimating quantities
Blocks are available in such a variety of sizes that in order to calculate the number required you must divide a given area of wall by the dimensions of a specific type of block. Blocks are sometimes specified in nominal sizes (larger than actual size) but with the $\frac{3}{8}$-inch allowance for mortar on the length and height only. Block walls are normally constructed with one skin of masonry, so the thickness of a block remains as the actual size.

Available sizes and designs
Standard blocks are nominally 16 inches long, 8 inches high and 8 inches thick. Many other sizes are available, as well, including half and three-quarter units. Available shapes vary widely: Units with keyed ends are used in ordinary wall construction, square-end blocks for corners. Single- and double-bullnose units can be used for decorative designs, and other blocks are designed for door jamb surrounds and lintels. There are also many decorative blocks, including pierced ornamental blocks and "tile" units.

Storing blocks
When blocks are delivered, have them unloaded as near as possible to the construction site to reduce the possibility of damage—they are brittle and chip easily. Stack them on a flat, dry base and protect them from rain and frost with a polyethylene tarpaulin.

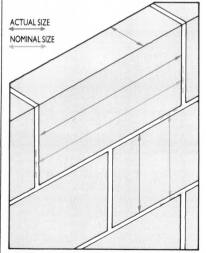

ACTUAL SIZE

NOMINAL SIZE

Sizes of structural blocks
The nominal size of a block refers to the length and height only. Thicknesses are always specified as an actual size.

SEE ALSO

Details for: ▷
Blocks — 22
Laying blocks — 36–37

BLOCKS AND STONES

Precast blocks made from poured concrete are available in a variety of colors, shapes and sizes. Aesthetically, however, nothing can surpass quarried stone such as granite or sandstone. Hewn roughly in natural shapes and textures, or as dressed blocks, natural stone is durable and weathers well.

Man-made concrete blocks
1 Solid, dense concrete
2 Lightweight
3 Lightweight aggregate
4 Pierced decorative
5 Solid decorative
6 Pitched-face reconstituted stone
7 Pilaster block
8 Pilaster coping
9 Multistone block
10 Screen coping
11 Split-face facing
12 Hewn-stone facing

Semidressed natural stone blocks

Dry-stone retaining wall

Split-stone walling

Knapped-flint boundary wall

CHOOSING NATURAL STONE

Practical considerations
In practical terms, the type of natural stone you choose for walls depends almost entirely on where you happen to live. In some parts of the country there are local restrictions governing the choice of building materials, and, in any case, a structure built from stone that is indigenous to a locality is more likely to blend sympathetically into its surroundings. Furthermore, buying stone from a local quarry makes economic sense—transporting stone over long distances can be very costly.

Where to obtain stone
If you live in a large town or city, obtaining natural stone can be a real problem. You might be prepared to buy a few small boulders for a rock garden from a local garden center, but the cost of buying enough stone for even a short run of walling is likely to be prohibitive. Masonry supply yards may carry some varieties of natural stone and can order others on your behalf, but transportation costs tend to inflate the price of the material.

Another source of materials, and possibly the cheapest way to obtain dressed stone, is to visit a demolition site. Prices vary considerably, but the cost of transport may be less than a supplier might offer.

Estimating quantities
As most quarries sell stone by the ton, it is difficult to estimate the quantity you need. Having worked out the approximate dimensions of the wall in question, telephone the nearest quarry for advice. Not only can you get an estimate of the cost of the stone, but you will be in a position to arrange for transport on your own.

Types of stone
Limestone, sandstone and granite are all suitable for building walls. Flint and slate require specialized building methods and are often used in combination with other materials. Stone bought in its natural state is classed as undressed; it is perfect for dry-stone walls in an informal garden. A more regular form of masonry is semidressed stone, which is cut into reasonably uniform blocks but with uneven surfaces, or fully dressed stone with machine-cut faces. The cost of stone increases in proportion to its preparation.

REPAIRING MASONRY

Cracks in external walls can be either the source of penetrating moisture (◁), which ruins your decoration inside, or the result of a much more serious problem: sinking of the foundations. Whatever the cause, it's obvious that you shouldn't just ignore the danger signs, but effect immediate cures.

Filling cracked masonry

If substantial cracks are apparent in a brick or stone wall, consult a builder or engineer to ascertain the cause.

If the crack seems to be stable, it can be filled. Where the crack follows the line of the mortar joints, rake out those affected and repoint in the normal way, as previously described. A crack that splits one or more bricks or stones cannot be repaired, and the damaged area should be removed and replaced, unless you are going to paint the wall afterwards.

Use a ready-mixed mortar with a little PVA bonding agent added to help it to stick. Soak the cracked masonry with a hose to encourage the mortar to flow deeply into the crack.

Crack may follow pointing only

Cracked bricks could signify serious faults

Priming brickwork

Brickwork will need to be primed only in certain circumstances. An alkali-resistant primer will guard against efflorescence (◁) and a stabilizing solution will bind crumbling masonry and help to seal it at the same time.

If you are planning to paint the wall for the first time with an exterior latex, you may find that the first coat is difficult to apply due to the suction of the dry, porous brick. Thin the first coat slightly with water.

To economize when using a thixotropic latex (◁), prime the wall with a cement paint with a little fine sand mixed in thoroughly.

Waterproofing masonry

Colorless water-repellent fluids are intended to make masonry impervious to water without coloring it or stopping it from breathing (important to allow moisture within the walls to dry out).

Prepare the surface thoroughly before applying the fluid; repair any cracks in bricks or pointing and remove organic growth (◁) and allow the wall to dry out thoroughly.

Apply the fluid generously with a large paintbrush and stipple it into the joints. Apply a second coat as soon as the first has been absorbed to ensure that there are no bare patches where water could seep in. To be sure that you're covering the wall properly, use a sealant containing a fugitive dye, which will disappear gradually after a few weeks.

Carefully paint up to surrounding woodwork; if you accidentally splash sealant onto it, wash it down immediately with a cloth dampened with solvent.

If the area you need to treat is large, consider spraying on the fluid, using a rented spray gun. You'll need to rig up a sturdy work platform (◁) and mask off all wood- and metalwork that adjoins the wall. The fumes from the fluid can be dangerous if inhaled, so be sure to wear a proper respirator, which you can also rent.

REPAIRING SPALLED MASONRY

Moisture penetrating soft masonry will expand in icy weather, flaking off the outer face of brickwork and stonework. The process, known as spalling, not only looks unattractive but also allows water to seep into the surface. Repairs to spalled bricks or stones can be made, although the treatment depends on the severity of the problem.

If spalling is localized, it is possible to cut out individual bricks or stones and replace them with matching ones. The sequence below describes how it's tackled with brickwork, but the process is similar for a stone wall.

Spalling bricks caused by frost damage

Where the spalling is extensive, it's likely that the whole wall is porous and your best remedy is to paint on a stabilizing solution to bind the loose material together, then apply a textured wall finish, as used to patch stucco, which will disguise the faults and waterproof the wall at the same time.

Replacing a spalled brick
Use a cold chisel and sledgehammer to rake out the pointing surrounding the brick, then chop out the brick itself. If the brick is difficult to pry out, drill into it many times with a large-diameter masonry bit, then attack the brick with a cold chisel and hammer. It should crumble, enabling you to remove the pieces easily.

To fit the replacement brick, first dampen the opening and spread mortar on the base and one side. Butter the dampened replacement brick on the top and one end and slot it into the hole (1).

Shape the pointing to match the surrounding brickwork then, once it is dry, apply a clear water repellent.

SEE ALSO

◁ Details for:

Organic growth	24
Efflorescence	24
Thixotropic latex	**77**

1 Replacing a spalled brick
Having mortared top and one end, slip the new brick into the hole you have cut.

CLEANING BRICK AND STONE

At regular intervals and before you decorate the outside of your house, check the condition of the brick and stonework, and carry out any necessary repairs. There's no reason why you can't paint brick or stone walls, but if you consider masonry most attractive in its natural state, you could be faced with a problem: once masonry is painted, it is difficult to restore it to its original condition. There will always be particles of paint left in the texture of brickwork, and even smooth stone, which can be stripped successfully, may be stained by the paint.

Stained brickwork

Organic growth

Efflorescence

Treating new masonry

New brickwork or stonework should be left for about three months until it is completely dry before any further treatment is considered. White, powdery deposits called efflorescence may come to the surface over this period, but you can simply brush it off with a stiff-bristled brush or a piece of burlap (◁). After that, bricks and mortar should be weatherproof and therefore require no further protection or treatment.

Cleaning organic growth from masonry

There are innumerable species of mold growth or lichens, which appear as tiny colored specks or patches on masonry. They gradually merge until the surface is covered with colors ranging from bright orange to yellow or green, gray and black.

Molds and lichen will flourish only in damp conditions, so try to cure the source of the problem before treating the growth. If one side of the house always faces away from the sun, it will have little chance to dry out. Relieve the situation by cutting back overhanging trees or shrubs to increase ventilation to the wall.

Make sure the earth surrounding masonry walls is graded so that surface water flows away from them.

Cracked or corroded downspouts leaking onto the wall are another common cause of organic growth. Feel behind the pipe with your fingers or use a hand mirror to locate the leak.

Removing the growth

Brush the wall vigorously with a stiff-bristled brush. This can be an unpleasant, dusty job, so wear a gauze facemask. Brush away from you to avoid debris being sprayed into your eyes.

Microscopic spores will remain even after brushing. Kill these with a solution of bleach or, if the wall suffers persistently from fungal growth, use a proprietary fungicide, available from most home centers.

Using a bleach solution

Mix one part household bleach with four parts water. Paint the solution onto the wall using an old paintbrush, then 48 hours later wash the surface with clean water, using a scrub brush. Brush on a second application of bleach solution if the original fungal growth was severe.

Using a fungicidal solution

Dilute the fungicide with water according to the manufacturer's instructions and apply it liberally to the wall with an old paintbrush. Leave it for 24 hours, then rinse the wall with clean water. In extreme cases, give the wall two washes of fungicide, allowing 24 hours between applications and a further 24 hours before washing it down with water.

Removing efflorescence from masonry

Soluble salts within building materials such as cement, brick, stone and plaster gradually migrate to the surface along with the water as a wall dries out. The result is a white crystalline deposit called efflorescence.

The same condition can occur on old masonry if it is subjected to more than average moisture. Efflorescence itself is not harmful, but the source of moisture causing it must be identified and cured if the surface is to remain unstained before painting.

Regularly brush the deposit from the wall with a dry stiff-bristled brush until the crystals cease to form—don't attempt to wash off the crystals; they'll merely dissolve in the water and soak back into the wall. Above all, don't attempt to paint a wall which is still efflorescing, and therefore damp.

When the wall is completely dry, paint the surface with an alkali-resistant primer to neutralize the effect of the crystals before you paint with oil paint; water-thinned paints or clear sealants let the wall breathe, so are not affected by the alkali content of the masonry. Most exterior latex paints can be used without primer (◁).

SUITABLE PAINTS FOR EXTERIOR MASONRY

There are various grades of paint suitable for decorating and protecting exterior masonry, which take into account economy, standard of finish, durability and coverage.

CEMENT PAINT

Cement paint is supplied as a dry powder, to which water is added. It is based on portland cement but pigments are added to produce a range of colors. Cement paint is the cheapest of the paints suitable for exterior use, although it is not as weatherproof as some others. Spray new or porous surfaces with water before you apply two coats.

Mixing cement paint
Shake or roll the container to loosen the powder, then add two parts powder to one of water in a clean bucket. Stir it to a smooth paste, then add a little more water until you achieve a full-bodied, creamy consistency. Mix up no more than you can use in one hour, or it will start to dry.

Adding an aggregate
When you're painting a dense wall or one treated with a stabilizing solution so that it its porosity is substantially reduced, it is advisable to add clean sand to the mix. It also provides added protection for an exposed wall and helps to cover dark colors. If the sand changes the color of the paint, add it to the first coat only. Use one part sand to four of powder, but stir it in when the paint is still in its pastelike consistency.

EXTERIOR LATEX

Exterior latex paint resembles the interior type; it is water-thinnable and dries to a similar smooth, flat finish. However, it is formulated to make it weatherproof and includes an additive to prevent organic growth; so apart from reinforced latexes, it is the only water-soluble paint that is recommended for use on outside walls.

The paint is ready for use, but thin the first coat on porous walls with 20 percent water. Follow up with one or two full-strength coats (depending on the color of the paint).

REINFORCED LATEX

Reinforced latex is a water-thinnable, resin-based paint to which has been added powdered mica or a similar fine aggregate. It dries with a textured finish that is extremely weatherproof, even in coastal districts or industrial areas and where darker colors are especially suitable. Although cracks and holes must be filled prior to painting, reinforced latex will cover hairline cracks and crazing. Apply two coats of paint in normal conditions, but you can economize by using sanded cement paint for the first coat.

SOLVENT-BASED MASONRY PAINT

A few masonry paints suitable for exterior walls are thinned with mineral spirits, but they are based on special resins so that, unlike most oil-based paints, they can be used on new walls without priming first with an alkali-resistant primer (▷). Check with manufacturer's recommendations. However, it is advisable to thin the first coat with 15 percent mineral spirits.

TEXTURED COATING

A thick textured coating can be applied to exterior walls. Such coatings are thoroughly weatherproof and often can be overpainted to match other colors. The usual preparation is necessary and brickwork should be pointed flush. Large cracks should be filled, but a textured coating will cover fine cracks. The paste is brushed or rolled onto the wall, then left to harden, forming an even texture. On the other hand, you can produce a texture of your choice using a variety of simple tools (▷). It's an easy process, but practice on a small section first.

Concrete floor paints

Floor paints are specially prepared to withstand hard wear. They are especially suitable for concrete garage or workshop floors, but they are also used for stone paving, steps and other concrete structures. They can be used inside for playroom floors.

The floor must be clean and dry and free from oil or grease. If the concrete is freshly laid, allow it to cure for at least three months before painting. Thin the first coat of paint with 10 percent mineral spirits.

Don't use floor paint over a surface sealed with a proprietary concrete sealer, but you can cover other paints so long as they are keyed first.

The best way to paint a large area is to use a paintbrush around the edges, then fit an extension to a paint roller for the bulk of the floor.

SEE ALSO

Details for: ▷
Preparing masonry   23–24

Apply paint with a roller on an extension

Paint in manageable sections
You can't hope to paint an entire house in one session, so divide each elevation into manageable sections to disguise the joints. The horizontal molding divide the wall neatly into two sections, and the raised door and window surrounds are convenient break lines.

TECHNIQUES FOR PAINTING MASONRY

SEE ALSO

◁ Details for:
Preparing masonry   23–24

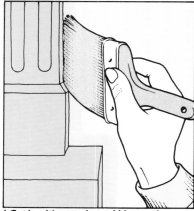

1 Cut in with a gentle scrubbing motion

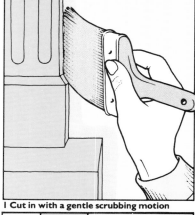

3 Use a banister brush
Tackle deeply textured wall surfaces with a banister brush, using a scrubbing action.

4 Use a roller
For speed in application, use a paint roller with a deep pile for heavy textures, a medium pile for light textures and smooth wall surfaces.

2 Protect the downspouts with newspaper

5 Spray onto the apex of external corners

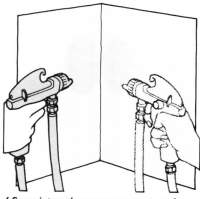

6 Spray internal corners as separate surfaces

Using paintbrushes

Choose a 4- to 6-inch-wide paintbrush for walls; larger ones are heavy and tiring to use. A good-quality brush with coarse bristles will last longer on rough walls. For a good coverage, apply the paint with vertical strokes, criss-crossed with horizontal ones. You will find it necessary to stipple paint into textured surfaces.

Cutting in
Painting up to a feature such as a door or window frame is known as cutting in. On a smooth surface, you should be able to paint a reasonably straight edge following the line of the feature, but it's difficult to apply the paint to a heavily textured wall with a normal brush stroke. Don't just apply more paint to overcome the problem; instead, touch the tip of the brush only to the wall, using a gentle scrubbing action (1), then brush excess paint away from the feature once the texture is filled.

Wipe splashed paint from window and door frames with a cloth dampened with the appropriate thinner.

Painting behind pipes
To protect rainwater downspouts, tape a roll of newspaper around them. Stipple behind the pipe with a brush, then slide the paper tube down the pipe to mask the next section (2).

Painting with a banister brush
Use a banister brush (3) to paint deeply textured masonry surfaces. Pour some paint into a roller tray and dab the brush in to load it. Scrub the paint onto the wall using circular strokes to work it well into the uneven surface.

Using a paint roller

A roller (4) will apply paint three times faster than a brush. Use a deep-pile roller for heavy textures or a medium-pile for lightly textured or smooth walls. Rollers wear quickly on rough walls, so have a spare sleeve handy. Vary the angle of the stroke when using a roller to ensure even coverage and use a brush to cut into angles and obstructions.

A paint tray is difficult to use at the top of a ladder, unless you fit a tool support or, better still, erect a flat platform to work from (◁).

Using a spray gun

Spraying is the quickest and most efficient way to apply paint to a large expanse of wall. But you will have to mask all the parts you do not want to paint, using newspaper and masking tape. The paint must be thinned by about 10 percent for spraying. Set the spray gun according to the manufacturer's instructions to suit the particular paint. It is advisable to wear a respirator when spraying.

Hold the gun about a foot away from the wall and keep it moving with even, parallel passes. Slightly overlap each pass and try to keep the gun pointing directly at the surface—tricky while standing on a ladder. Trigger the gun just before each pass and release it at the end of the stroke.

When spraying a large, blank wall, paint it into vertical bands, overlapping each band about 4 inches.

Spray external corners by aiming the gun directly at the apex so that paint falls evenly on both surfaces (5). When two walls meet at an internal angle, treat each surface separately (6).

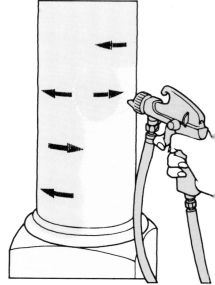

Spray-painting columns
Columns, part of a front door portico, for instance, should be painted in a series of overlapping vertical bands. Apply the bands by running the spray gun from side to side as you work down the column.

MORTAR FOR MASONRY WALLS

When building a wall, mortar is used to bind together the bricks, concrete blocks or stones. The durability of a masonry structure depends on the quality of the mortar used in its construction. If it is mixed correctly to the right consistency, the mortar will become as hard and strong as the masonry itself, but if the ingredients are added in the wrong proportions, the mortar will be weak and prone to cracking. If too much water is used, the mortar will be squeezed out of the joints by the weight of the masonry, and if the mortar is too dry, adhesion will be poor.

The ingredients of mortar

The ingredients of general-purpose mortar are portland cement, hydrated lime and sand, mixed with enough water to make a workable paste.

Cement is the hardening agent which binds the other ingredients together. The lime slows down the drying process and prevents the mortar setting too quickly. It also makes the mix flow well so that it fills gaps in the masonry and adheres to the texture of blocks or bricks. The sand acts as fine aggregate, adding body to the mortar, and reduces the possibility of shrinkage.

Use fine builders' sand for general-purpose mortar. However, use silver sand if you want a paler mortar to bond white screen blocks.

Plasticizers

If you are laying masonry in cold weather, substitute a proprietary plasticizer for the lime. Plasticizer produces aerated mortar—the tiny air bubbles in the mix allow the water to expand in freezing conditions and reduce the risk of cracking. Premixed masonry cement, with an aerating agent, is ready for mixing with sand.

Ready-mix mortar

Ready-mix mortar contains all the essential ingredients mixed to the correct proportions. You simply add water. It is a more expensive way of buying mortar but convenient to use and is available in small quantities.

SEE ALSO

Details for: ▷

Cutting bricks   30

Mixing mortar

Mortar must be used within two hours of mixing or be discarded, so make only as much as you can use within that time. An average of about two minutes to lay one brick is a reasonable estimate.

Choose a flat site upon which to mix the materials—a sheet of plywood will do—and dampen it slightly to prevent its absorbing water from the mortar. Make a pile of half the amount of sand to be used, then add the other ingredients. Put the rest of the sand on top, and mix the dry materials thoroughly.

Scoop a depression in the pile and add clean tap water. Never use contaminated or salty water. Push the dry mix from around the edge of the pile into the water until it has absorbed enough for you to blend the mix with a shovel, using a chopping action. Add more water, little by little, until the mortar has a butterlike consistency, slipping easily from the shovel but firm enough to hold its shape if you make a hollow in the mix. If the sides of the hollow collapse, add more dry ingredients until the mortar firms up. Make sure the mortar is not too dry or it won't form a strong bond with the masonry.

If mortar stiffens up while you are working, add just enough water to restore the consistency. Dampen the mixing board again.

Correct consistency
The mortar mix should be firm enough to hold its shape when you make a depression in the mix.

Proportions for masonry mixes

Mix the ingredients according to the prevailing conditions at the building site. Use a general-purpose mortar for moderate conditions where the wall is reasonably sheltered, but use a stronger mix for severe conditions where the wall will be exposed to wind and driving rain, or if the site is elevated or near the coast. If you are using plasticizer instead of lime, follow the manufacturer's instructions regarding the quantity you should add to the sand.

● **Estimating quantity**
As a rough guide to estimating how much mortar you will need, allow approximately 1 cu. yd. of sand (other ingredients in proportion) to lay: 1600 to 1650 bricks; 69 to 70 sq. yds. average facing blocks; 100 to 105 sq. yds. screen or structural blocks.

BRICKLAYERS' TERMS

Bricklayers use a number of specialized words and phrases to describe their craft and materials. Terms used frequently are listed below while others are described as they occur.

BRICK FACES *The surfaces of a brick.*
Stretcher faces The long sides of a brick.
Header faces The short ends of a brick.
Bedding faces The top and bottom surfaces.
Frog The depression in one bedding face.

COURSES *The individual, horizontal rows of bricks.*
Stretcher course A single course with stretcher faces visible.
Header course A single course with header faces visible.
Coping The top course designed to protect the wall from rainwater.
Bond Pattern produced by staggering alternate courses so that vertical joints are not aligned one above the other.
Stretcher A single brick from a stretcher course.
Header A single brick from a header course.
Closure brick The last brick laid in a course.

CUT BRICKS *Bricks cut with a bolster chisel to even up the bond.*
Bat A brick cut across its width, e.g. half-bat, three-quarter bat.
Queen closer A brick cut along its length.

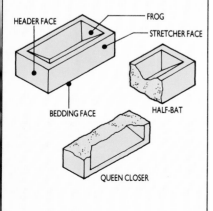

HEADER FACE — FROG
— STRETCHER FACE
BEDDING FACE
HALF-BAT
QUEEN CLOSER

MORTAR MIXING PROPORTIONS

	Cement/lime mortar	Plasticized mortar	Masonry cement mortar
General-purpose mortar (Moderate conditions)	1 part cement 1 part lime 6 parts sand	1 part cement 6 parts sand/ plasticizer	1 part cement 5 parts sand
Strong mortar (Severe conditions)	1 part cement ½ part lime 4 parts sand	1 part cement 4 parts sand/ 3 parts sand plasticizer	1 part cement 3 parts sand

DESIGNING A WALL FOR STABILITY

It is easy enough to appreciate the loads and stresses imposed upon the walls of a house or outbuilding, and therefore the necessity for solid foundations and adequate methods of reinforcement and protection to prevent their collapsing. It is not so obvious, but even a simple garden wall requires similar measures to ensure its stability. It is merely irritating if a low dividing wall or planter falls apart, but a serious injury could result from the collapse of a heavy boundary wall.

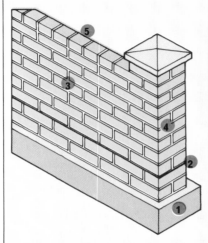

The basic structure of a wall
Unless you design and build a wall in the correct manner, it will not be strong and stable.

1 Footings
A wall must be built upon a solid concrete platform known as a strip footing. The dimensions of the footing vary according to the height and weight of the wall.

2 Damp-proof course
A layer of waterproof material 6 inches above ground level stops water from rising from the soil. It is not needed for most garden walling unless it abuts a building with a similar DPC. Not only does it protect the house from dampness, but it reduces the likelihood of freezing water expanding and cracking the joints.

3 Bonding
The staggered pattern of bricks is not merely decorative. It is designed to spread the static load along the wall and to tie the individual units together.

4 Piers
Straight walls over a certain height and length must be buttressed at regular intervals with thick columns of brickwork known as piers. They resist the sideways pressure caused by high winds.

5 Coping
The coping prevents frost damage by shedding rainwater from the top of the wall where it could seep into the upper brick joints.

BONDING BRICKWORK

Mortar is extremely strong under compression, but its tensile strength is relatively weak. If bricks were stacked one upon the other so that the vertical joints were continuous, any movement within the wall would pull them apart and the structure would be seriously weakened. Bonding brickwork staggers the vertical joints, transmitting the load along the entire length of the wall. Try out the bond of your choice by dry-laying a few bricks before you embark on the actual building work.

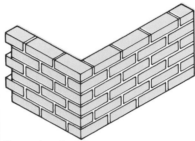

Stretcher bond
The stretcher bond is the simplest form of bonding, used for single-thickness walls, including the two individual leaves of a cavity wall found in the construction of modern buildings. Half-bats are used to make the bond at the end of a straight wall, while a corner is formed by alternating headers and stretchers.

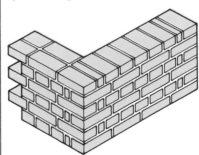

English bond
If you build an 8-inch-thick wall by laying courses of stretcher-bonded bricks side by side, there would be a weak vertical joint running centrally down the wall. An English bond strengthens the wall by using alternate courses of headers. Staggered joints are maintained at the end of a wall and at a corner by inserting a queen closer before the last header.

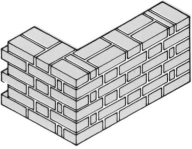

Flemish bond
The Flemish bond is an alternative method to English bond for building a solid, 8-inch-thick wall. Every course is laid with alternate headers and stretchers. Stagger the joint at the end of a course and at a corner by laying a queen closer before the header.

Decorative bonds
Stretcher, English and Flemish bonds are designed to construct strong walls—decorative qualities are incidental. Other bonds, used primarily for their visual effect, are suitable for low, nonload-bearing walls only, supported by a conventionally bonded base and piers.

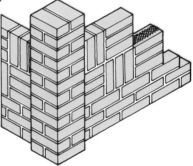

Stack bonding
A basketweave effect is achieved by stack bonding bricks in groups of three. Strengthen the continuous vertical joints with wall ties (◁).

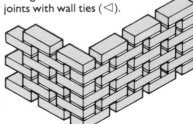

Honeycomb bond
Build an open, decorative screen using a stretcherlike bond with a quarter-bat-size space between each brick. Build the screen carefully to keep the bond regular, and cut quarter-bats to fill the gaps in the top course.

CONSTRUCTING STRIP FOOTINGS

Stringent code regulations govern the size and reinforcement required for the footings to support high and especially *structural walls, but most garden walls can be built upon concrete footings laid in a straight-sided trench.*

Size of footings

The footings must be sufficiently substantial to support the weight of the wall, and the soil must be firm and well drained to avoid possible subsidence. It is unwise to set footings in ground which has been filled recently, such as a new building site. Also, take care to avoid tree roots and drainpipes. If the trench begins to fill with water as you are digging, seek professional advice before proceeding.

Dig the trench deeper than the footing itself so that the first one or two courses of brick are below ground level. This will allow for an adequate depth of soil for planting right up to the wall.

If the soil is not firmly packed when you reach the required depth, dig deeper until you reach a firm level, then fill the bottom of the trench with compacted hardcore up to the lowest level of the proposed footing.

RECOMMENDED DIMENSIONS FOR FOOTINGS

Type of wall	Height of wall	Depth of footing	Width of footing
One brick thick	3 ft.	4 to 6 in.	12 in.
Two bricks thick	3 ft.	9 to 12 in.	18 in.
Two bricks thick	3 to 6 ft.	16 to 18 in.	18 to 24 in.
Retaining wall	3 ft.	6 to 12 in.	16 to 18 in.

Setting out the footings

For a straight footing, set up two form boards made from 2-inch-thick (nominal) lumber nailed to stakes driven into the ground at each end of the proposed trench but well outside the work area.

Drive nails into the top edge of each board and strentch lines between them to mark the front and back edges of the wall. Then drive nails into the form boards on each side of the wall line to indicate the width of the footings, and stretch more lines between them (**1**).

When you are satisfied that the setting out is accurate, remove the lines marking the wall but leave the nails in place so that you can replace the lines when you come to lay the bricks.

Place a level against the remaining lines to mark the edge of the footing on the ground (**2**). Mark the ends of the footing extending beyond the line of the wall by half the wall's thickness. Mark the edge of the trench on the ground with a spade and remove the lines. Leave the boards in place.

Turning corners

If your wall will have a right-angled corner, set up two sets of form boards as before, checking carefully that the lines form a true right angle using the 3:4:5 right triangle method (**3**).

Digging the trench

Excavate the trench, keeping the sides vertical, and check that the bottom is level, using a long, straight piece of wood and a level.

Drive a stake into the bottom of the trench near one end until the top of the stake represents the depth of the footing. Drive in more stakes at 3-foot intervals, checking that the tops are level (**4**).

Filling the trench

Pour a foundation mix of concrete ($\triangleright$) into the trench, then tamp it down firmly with a heavy piece of lumber until it is exactly level with the top of the stakes. Leave the stakes in place and allow the footing to harden thoroughly before building the wall.

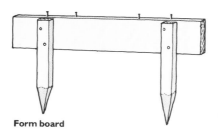

Form board

FOOTING FOR A SLOPING SITE

When the ground slopes gently, simply ignore the gradient and make the footing perfectly level. If the site slopes noticeably, make a stepped footing by placing plywood form stops across the trench at regular intervals. Calculate the height and length of the steps using multiples of normal brick size.

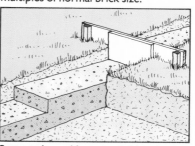

Support plywood form stops with stakes

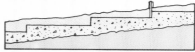

Section through a stepped footing
A typical stepped concrete footing with one of the plywood form stops in place.

SEE ALSO

Details for: ▷	
Level	30
Concrete mixes	43

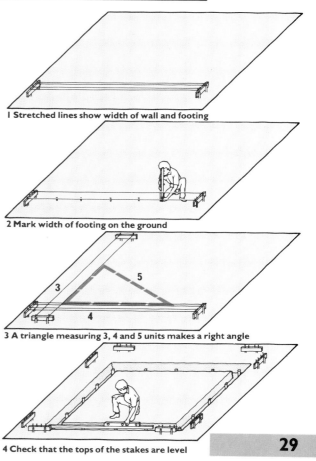

1 Stretched lines show width of wall and footing

2 Mark width of footing on the ground

3 A triangle measuring 3, 4 and 5 units makes a right angle

4 Check that the tops of the stakes are level

BRICKLAYING TOOLS

You can make or improvise some builder's tools (◁) but you will have to buy some of the more-specialized bricklayer's tools.

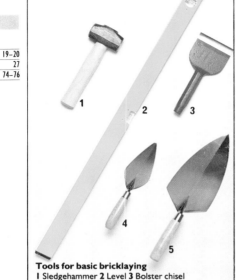

Tools for basic bricklaying
1 Sledgehammer 2 Level 3 Bolster chisel
4 Pointing trowel 5 Brick trowel

LAYING BRICKS

Spreading a bed of mortar—throwing a line—requires practice before you can develop speed, so concentrate at first on laying bricks neatly and accurately. Mortar mixed to the right consistency (◁) helps to keep the visible faces of the bricks clean. In hot, dry weather, dampen the footings and bricks, but let any surface water evaporate before you begin to lay bricks.

Bricklaying techniques

Hold the brick trowel with your thumb in line with the handle, pointing towards the tip of the blade (1).

Scoop a measure of mortar out of the pile and shape it roughly to match the shape of the trowel blade. Pick up the mortar by sliding the blade under the pile, setting it onto the trowel with a slight jerk of the wrist (2).

Spread the mortar along the top course by aligning the edge of the trowel with the center line of the bricks. As you tip the blade to deposit the mortar, draw the trowel back towards you to stretch the bed over at least two to three bricks (3).

Furrow the mortar by pressing the point of the trowel along the center (4).

Pick up a brick with your other hand, but don't extend your thumb too far onto the stretcher face or it will disturb the builders' line every time you place a brick in position. Press the brick into the bed, picking up excess mortar squeezed from the joint by sliding the edge of the trowel along the wall (5).

With the mortar picked up on the trowel, butter the header of the next brick, making a neat 1/8-inch bed for the header joint (6). Press the brick against its neighbor, scooping off excess mortar with the trowel.

Having laid three bricks, use the level to make sure they are horizontal. Make any adjustments by tapping them down with the trowel handle (7).

Hold the level along the outer edge of the bricks to check that they are in line. To move a brick sideways without knocking it off its mortar bed, tap the upper edge with the trowel at about 45 degrees (8).

1 The correct way to hold a brick trowel

Cutting bricks
To cut bricks use a bolster to mark the line on all faces by tapping gently with a hammer. Realign the blade on the visible stretcher face and strike the chisel firmly.

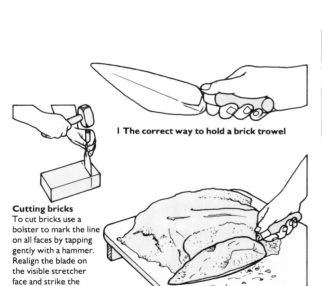

2 Scoop a measure of mortar onto the trowel

3 Stretch a bed of mortar along the course

5 Push down brick and remove excess mortar

7 Level the course of bricks with the trowel

6 Butter the head of the next brick

4 Furrow the mortar with the trowel point

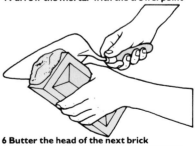

8 Tap the bricks sideways to align them

BUILDING A STRETCHER-BONDED WALL

A single-width brick wall looks unsubstantial and, over a certain height, is structurally weak unless it is supported with piers or changes direction by forming right-angle corners. In any case, the ability to construct strong, accurate corners is a requirement for building most structures, including simple garden planters. Building a wall with another type of bond is a little more complicated in detail (▷), but the basic construction principles remain the same.

Setting out the corners

Mark out the footings and face of the wall by stretching string lines between profile boards (▷). When the footings have been filled and the concrete has set, use a plumb line or hold a level lightly against the line to mark the corners and the face of the wall on the footing (1). Join the marks with a pencil and straightedge, and check the accuracy of the corners with a builder's square. Stretch a line between the corner marks to check the alignment.

Building the corners

Build the corners first as a series of steps or "leads" before filling between. It is essential that they form true right angles, so take your time.

Throw a bed of mortar, then lay three bricks in both directions against the marked line. Check that they are level in all directions, including across the diagonal, by laying a level between the end bricks (2).

Build the leads to a height of five stepped courses, using a gauge stick to measure the height of each course as you proceed (3). Use alternate headers and stretchers to form the actual point of the corner.

Use a level to plumb the corner, and check the alignment of the stepped bricks by holding the level against the side of the wall (4).

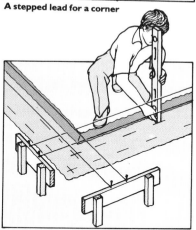

A stepped lead for a corner

I Mark the face of the wall on the footing

• **Covering the wall**
Cover finished or partly built walls overnight with sheets of polyethylene or tarpaulin to protect the brickwork from rain or frost. Weight the edges of the covers with bricks.

2 Level the first course of bricks

3 Check the height with a gauge stick

4 Check that the steps are in line

Building the straight sections

Stretch a builder's line between the corners so that it aligns perfectly with the top edge of the first course (5).

Lay the first straight course of bricks from both ends toward the middle. As you near the middle point, lay the last few bricks dry to make certain they will fit. Then mortar them in, finishing with the central or "closure" brick. Spread mortar onto both ends of the closure brick and onto the header faces of the bricks on each side. Lay the closure brick very carefully (6), and scoop off excess mortar with the trowel.

Lay subsequent courses between the leaders in the same way, raising the builder's line each time. To build the wall higher, raise the corners first by constructing leads to the required height, then fill the spaces between.

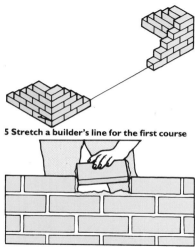

5 Stretch a builder's line for the first course

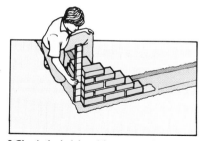

6 Carefully lay the last or closure brick

• **Building a straight wall**
To build a straight wall without a corner, follow the procedure described left, building end leads—straight stepped sections—at each end of the wall, then fill between with bricks.

Coping the wall
You could finish the wall by laying the last course frog downwards, but a coping of half-bats laid on end looks more professional. Alternatively, use proprietary coping bricks or blocks (▷).

POINTING BRICKWORK

Finishing the mortar joints—pointing—compresses the materials to make a packed, watertight joint and enhances the appearance of the wall. Well-struck joints and clean brickwork are essential if the wall is to look professionally built, but the mortar must be shaped at the right time for best results.

Flush joint

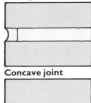

Concave joint

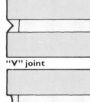

"V" joint

Raked joint

Weather joint

Colored mortar
You can add colored powders to your mortar mix. Make a trial batch to test the color when dry. Rake out the joint and apply with a tray to avoid staining the bricks.

Mortar for pointing work

If the mortar is still too wet, the joint will not be crisp and you may drag mortar out from between the bricks. On the other hand, if it is left to harden too long, pointing will be hard work and you may leave dark marks on the joint.

Test the consistency of the mortar by pressing your thumb into a joint. If it holds a clear impression without sticking to your thumb the mortar is just right for pointing. Because it is so important that you shape the joint at exactly the right moment, you may have to point the work in stages before you can complete the wall.

Shape the joints to match existing brickwork or choose one that is suitable for the prevailing weather conditions.

How to make pointing joints

Flush joint
Rub a piece of sacking along each joint to finish the mortar flush with the bricks. This is a utilitarian joint for a wall built with second-hand bricks which are not of a sufficiently good quality to take a crisp joint.

Concave joint
Buy a shaped jointing tool to make a concave joint, or improvise with a length of bent tubing. Flush the mortar first, then drag the tool along the joints. Finish the vertical joints, then do the long, continuous horizontal ones.

Shape the mortar with a jointing tool

"V" joint
Produced in a similar way to the concave joint, the "V" joint gives a very smart finish to new brickwork and sheds rainwater well.

Raked joint
Use a piece of wood or metal to rake out the joints to a depth of about 1/4 inch, then compress them again by smoothing the mortar lightly with a piece of rounded dowel rod. Raked joints do not shed water so don't use them on an exposed site.

Weather joint
The angled weather joint is ideal, even in harsh conditions. Use a small pointing trowel to shape the vertical joints (1). They can slope to the left or right, but be consistent throughout the same section of brickwork. Shape the horizontal joints allowing the mortar to spill out slightly at the base of each joint. Professionals finish the joint by cutting off excess mortar with a tool called a Frenchman, similar to a table knife with the tip at 90 degrees. Improvise a similar tool with a strip of bent metal. Align a straightedge with the bottom of the joint to guide the tool and produce a neat, straight edge to the mortar. Nail two scraps of plywood to the guide to hold it away from the wall (2).

1 Shape the weather joint with a trowel

2 Remove excess mortar with a Frenchman

Brushing the brickwork
Let the shaped joints harden a little before you clean scraps of mortar from the face of the wall. Use a medium-soft brush, sweeping lightly across the joints so as not to damage them.

COPINGS FOR BRICK WALLS

The coping, which forms the top course of the wall, protects the brickwork from weathering and gives a finished appearance to the wall. Strictly speaking, if the coping is flush with both faces of the wall, it is a capping. A true coping projects from the face so that water drips clear and does not stain the brickwork.

You can lay a coping of bricks with their stretcher faces across the width of the wall. Use the same type of brick employed in the construction of the wall or specially shaped coping bricks designed to shed rainwater. Engineering bricks are sometimes used for copings. The dense water-resistant quality of the brick is an advantage and the color makes a pleasing contrast with regular brickwork.

Stone or cast concrete slabs are popular for garden walls. They are quick to lay and are wide enough to form low, bench-type seating.

On an exposed site, consider installing a damp-proof course (◁) under the coping to reduce the risk of frost attack. Use a standard bituminous felt DPC or lay two courses of plain roof tiles with staggered joints and a brick coping above. Let the tiles project from the face of the wall but run a sloping mortar joint along the top of the projection to shed water.

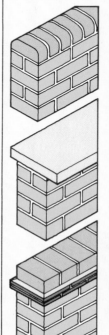

Brick coping
Specially shaped bricks are made to cope a wall.

Slab coping
Choose a concrete or stone slab that is wider than the wall itself.

Tile and brick coping
Lay flat roof tiles or specially made creasing tiles beneath a brick coping to form a weatherproof layer which allows water to drip clear of the wall.

BUILDING INTERSECTING WALLS

When building new garden walls which intersect at right angles, either anchor them by bonding the brickwork (see below), or take the easier option to link them with wall ties at every third course (▷). If the intersecting wall is over 6 feet in length, make the junction a control joint by using straight metal strips as wall ties (▷).

Building up to an existing wall

When you build a new wall to intersect the existing wall of a house, you must include a damp-proof course to prevent water from bridging the house DPC via the new masonry (▷) and you must make a positive joint between the two walls.

Inserting a DPC

Good building practice requires a damp-proof course in all masonry construction to prevent rising dampness. This consists of a layer of impervious material built into the mortar bed about 6 inches above ground level. When you build a new wall, its DPC must coincide with the DPC in the existing structure. Use a roll of bituminous felt chosen to match the thickness of the new wall.

Locate the house DPC and build the first few courses of the new wall up to that level. Spread a thin bed of mortar on the bricks and lay the DPC upon it with the end of the roll turned up against the existing wall (**1**). The next course of bricks will trap the DPC between the header joint and the wall. Lay more mortar on top of the DPC to produce the standard ⅜-inch joint ready for laying the next course in the normal way. If you have to join rolls of DPC, overlap the ends by 6 inches.

Tying in the new wall

The traditional method for linking a new wall with an existing structure involves chopping recesses in the brickwork at every fourth course. End bricks of the new wall are set into the recesses, bonding the two structures together (**2**). An alternative and much simpler method, however, is to screw a special stainless metal channel to the wall, designed to accept bricks or concrete blocks and provide anchoring points for standard wire wall ties (▷). Channels are available for masonry units in standard sizes.

Screw the channel to the old wall above the DPC with stainless-steel lag screws and wall plugs or use expanding bolts (**3**). Though not essential, trap 3 feet of DPC felt behind the channel.

Mortar the end of a brick before feeding it into the channel (**4**). As the brick is pushed home, the mortar squeezes through the perforated channel to make a firm bond.

At every third course, hook a wall tie over the pressed lugs in the channel and bed it firmly into the mortar joint (**5**).

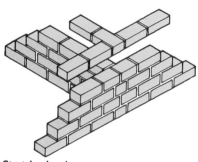

Stretcher bond

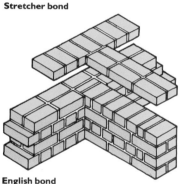

English bond

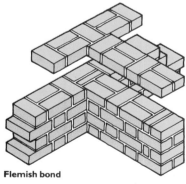

Flemish bond

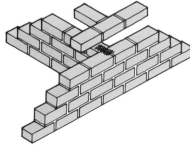

Using a wall tie

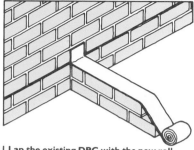

1 Lap the existing DPC with the new roll

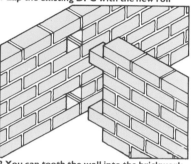

2 You can tooth the wall into the brickwork

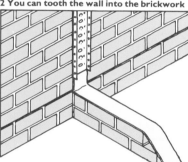

3 But it is easier to use a special channel

4 Locate the brick ends in the channel

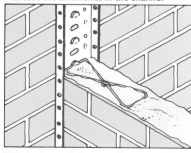

5 Hook wire wall ties over the pressed lugs

DPC on a sloping site
When the site slopes noticeably, the wall footing is stepped to keep the top of the wall level (▷). If you include a DPC in the wall, that, too, must follow the line of the steps to keep it the required height above ground level.

BRICKWORK PIERS

A pier is a free-standing column of masonry used to support a porch. It can be used as an individual gatepost as well. When it is built as part of a wall, it is more accurately termed a pilaster. In practice, however, the word "column" often covers either description. Columns bonded into a masonry base but extending up each side of a wooden trellis to support a pergola is a typical example. To avoid confusion, any supporting brick column will be described here as a pier. Thorough planning is essential when building piers.

Structural considerations

Any free-standing straight wall over a certain length and height must be buttressed at regular intervals by piers. Wall sections and piers must be tied together, either by a brick bond or by inserting metal wall ties in every third course of bricks. Any single-width brick wall, whatever its height, would benefit from supporting piers at open ends and gateways where it is most vulnerable; these will also improve the appearance of the wall. Piers over 3 feet, and especially those supporting gates, should be built around steel reinforcing rods set in the concrete footings. Whether reinforcing is included or not, allow for the size of piers when designing the footings (◁).

Designing the piers

Piers should be placed no more than 10 feet apart in walls over a certain height (see chart). The wall itself can be flush with one face of a pier, but the entire structure is stronger if it is centered on the column.

Piers should be a minimum of twice the thickness of a 3¾-inch-thick wall, but build 1-foot-square piers when reinforcement is required, including gateways, and to buttress 8-inch-thick walls.

INCORPORATING PIERS IN A BRICK WALL

Thickness of wall	Maximum height without piers	Maximum pier spacing
3¾ in.	1 ft. 6 in.	10 ft.
8 in.	4 ft. 6 in.	10 ft.

BONDING PIERS

If you prefer the appearance of bonded brick piers, construct them as shown below, but it is easier, especially when building walls centered on piers, to use wall ties to reinforce continuous vertical joints in the brickwork.

Various types of galvanized metal wall ties are available. Wire is bent into a butterfly shape **(1)**. Stamped metal steel strips have forked ends and are known as "fish tails" **(2)**. Expanded metal mesh is cut in straight strips **(3)**.

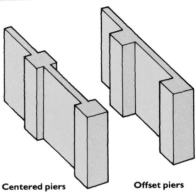

Centered piers   **Offset piers**

- **Bonding piers**
  It is simpler to tie any wall to a pier with wall ties (see above right) but it is relatively easy to bond a pier into a single-brick width wall.

Color key
You will have to cut certain bricks to bond a pier into a straight wall. Whole bricks are colored with a light tone, three-quarter bats with a medium tone, and half-bats with a dark tone.

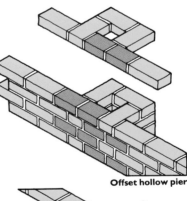

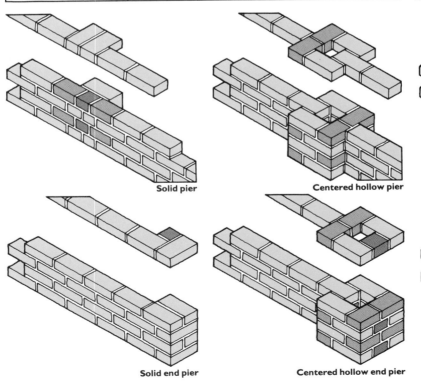

Solid pier   **Centered hollow pier**   **Offset hollow pier**

Solid end pier   **Centered hollow end pier**   **Offset hollow end pier**

BUILDING PIERS

Mark out accurately the positions of piers and the face of the wall on the concrete footing (▷). Lay the first course for the piers using a builder's line stretched between two stakes to align them (**1**). Adjust the position of the line if necessary, and fill in between with the first straight course working from both ends toward the middle (**2**). Build alternate pier and wall courses, checking the level and the vertical faces and corners of the piers. At the third course, push metal wall ties into the mortar bed to span the joint between wall and pier (**3**). Continue in the same way to the required height of the wall, then raise the piers to their required height (**4**). Lay a coping along the wall and cap the piers with concrete or stone slabs (**5**).

1 Lay pier bases
Stretch a builder's line to position the bases of the piers.

2 Lay first wall course
Move the line to keep the first course straight.

3 Lay pier ties
Tie the piers to the wall by inserting wall ties into every third course. Put a tile into alternate courses for a gate-supporting pier.

4 Raise the piers
Build the piers higher than the wall to allow for a decorative coping along the top course.

5 Lay the coping
Lay the coping slabs and cap the piers.

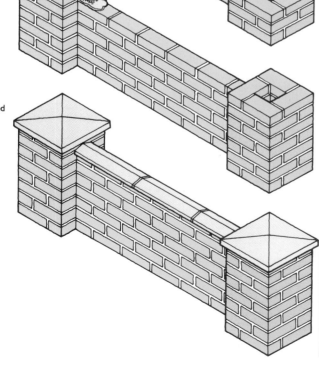

Incorporating control joints

Although you would never notice, a brick wall is constantly moving due to ground settlement as well as expansion and contraction of the materials. Over short distances, the movement is so slight that it hardly affects the brickwork, but the combined movement of masonry in a long wall can crack the structure. To compensate for this movement, build unmortared, continuous vertical joints into a wall at intervals of about 20 feet. These control joints can be placed in a straight section of wall, but it is neater and more convenient to place them where the wall meets a pier. Build the pier and wall as normal, but omit the mortar from the header joints of the wall. Instead of inserting standard wall ties, embed a flat, 1/8-inch-thick galvanized strip in the mortar bed. Lightly grease one half of the strip so that it can slide lengthwise to allow for movement yet still key the wall and pier together. When the wall is complete, fill the joint from both sides with mastic.

Incorporating reinforcement

Use 5/8-inch steel reinforcing bars to strengthen brick piers. If the pier is under 3 feet in height, use one continuous length of bar (**1**), but for taller piers, embed a bent starter bar in the footing, projecting a minimum of 24 inches above the level of the concrete (**2**). As the work proceeds, bind extension bars to the projection with galvanized wire up to within 2 inches of the top of the pier. Fill in around the reinforcement with concrete as you build the pier, but pack it carefully, trying not to disturb the brickwork.

SEE ALSO.

Details for: ▷	
Bricks	19–20
Laying bricks	30–31
Marking out	31
Wall ties	34
Mixing concrete	41

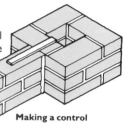

Making a control joint
Tie the pier to the wall with galvanized-metal strips when making a control joint (shown here before it's set in mortar). The mastic is squeezed into the joint between the wall and the pier.

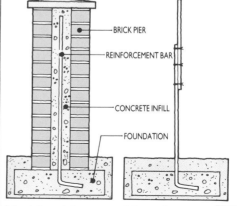

BRICK PIER

REINFORCEMENT BAR

CONCRETE INFILL

FOUNDATION

1 A reinforced pier   **2 Starter bar**

BUILDING WITH CONCRETE BLOCKS

● **Building piers**
High, free-standing garden walls constructed from blocks must be supported by piers at 10-foot intervals (◁).

The methods for laying concrete blocks are much the same as for building with bricks. Block walls need similar concrete footings, and the same type of mortar, although heavy blocks should be laid with a strong, firm mix (◁) to resist the additional weight of the freshly constructed wall. As blocks are made in a greater variety of sizes, you can build a wall of any thickness with a simple stretcher bond (◁). However, don't dampen concrete blocks before laying them—wet blocks can shrink and crack the mortar joints as the wall dries out. When you are building decorative walls with facing blocks, use any of the pointing styles described for bricks (◁), but flush-joint a wall built with structural blocks which is to be stuccoed.

CONTROL JOINTS

Walls over 20 feet in length should be built with a continuous, vertical control joint to allow for expansion (◁). Place an unmortared joint in a straight section of wall or against a pier, and bridge the gap with galvanized-metal dowels as for brickwork (◁). Fill the gap with mastic.

It is unlikely, but if you need to insert a control joint in a dividing wall, form the joint between the door frame and wall. In this case, fill the joints with mortar in the normal way but rake them out to a depth of ¾ inch around one end of the lintel and vertically to the ceiling on both sides of the wall. Fill the control joint flush with mastic.

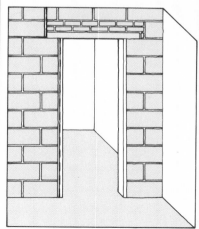

A control joint next to a door opening
Take the joint around the lintel and up to the ceiling on both sides of the wall.

Building a dividing wall

Building a nonload-bearing stud partition (◁) is the usual method for dividing up a large internal space into smaller rooms, but if your house is built on a concrete pad, a practical alternative is to use concrete blocks. If you install a doorway in the dividing wall, plan its position to avoid cutting too many blocks. Allow for the wooden door frame and lining (◁) as well as a precast lintel to support the masonry above the opening (◁). Fill the space above the lintel with cut blocks or bricks to level the courses.

Screw galvanized pressed-metal channels (◁) to the existing structure to support each end of the dividing wall. Plumb them accurately or the new wall will be out of true. Lay the first course of blocks without mortar across the room to check their spacing and the position of a doorway if one is to be included. Mark the positions of the blocks before building stepped leads at each end as for brickwork (◁). Check for accuracy with a level. Fill between the leads with blocks.

Build another three courses, anchoring the end blocks to the channels with wall ties in every joint. Leave the mortar to harden overnight before you continue with the wall.

Building a dividing wall

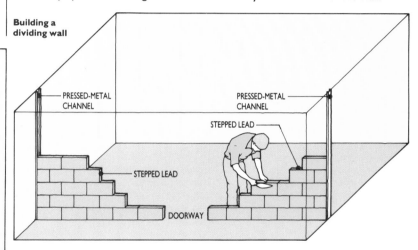

PRESSED-METAL CHANNEL

PRESSED-METAL CHANNEL

STEPPED LEAD

STEPPED LEAD

DOORWAY

Building intersecting walls

Butt intersecting garden walls together with a continuous vertical joint between them, but anchor the structure as for brickwork (◁) with wire-mesh wall ties (**1**). If you build a wall with heavy, but hollow, blocks, use stout metal tie bars with a bend at each end. Fill the block cores with mortar to embed the ends of the bars (**2**). Install a tie in every course.

1 Wire-mesh wall tie for solid blocks ▶
2 Metal tie bar for hollow blocks

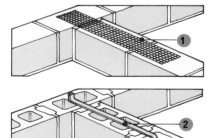

Cutting blocks

Use a bolster chisel and straightedge to score or cut a line around a block. Deepen the groove by tapping the chisel with a hammer. The chisel will ring with each blow until a crack makes its way through the block with a dull thud. One more sharp blow should split the block.

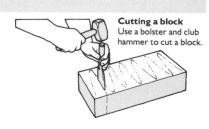

Cutting a block
Use a bolster and club hammer to cut a block.

BUILDING A DECORATIVE BLOCK SCREEN

Basic bricklaying techniques and tools (▷) are used to build a pierced concrete screen, but because the blocks are stack-bonded—with continuous vertical joints—the wall must be reinforced vertically with ⅝-inch steel bars, and horizontally with galvanized mesh if it is built higher than 2 feet. Build the screen with supporting piers located no more than 10 feet apart using matching pilaster blocks. Or you might prefer the appearance of contrasting masonry; in that case, construct a base and piers from bricks or facing blocks.

Constructing the screen

Set out and fill the footings (▷) twice the width of the pilaster blocks. Embed pier reinforcing bars in the concrete (◁) and support them with guy ropes until the concrete sets.

Lower a pilaster block over the first bar, setting it onto a bed of mortar laid around the base of the bar. Check that the block is perfectly vertical and level, and that its locating channel faces the next pier. Pack mortar or concrete into its core, then proceed with two more blocks so that the pier corresponds to the height of two mortared screen blocks (**1**). Construct each pier in the same way. Intermediate piers will have a locating channel on each side.

Allow the mortar to harden overnight, then lay a mortar bed for two screen blocks next to the first pair. Butter the vertical edge of a screen block and press it into the pier locating channel (**2**). Tap it into the mortar bed and check it is level. Mortar the next block and place it alongside the first.

When buttering screen blocks, take special care to keep the faces clean by making a neat, chamfered bed of mortar on each block (**3**).

Lay two more blocks against the next pier, stretch a builder's line to gauge the top edge of the first course, and then lay the rest of the blocks toward the center. Lay the second course in the same way, making sure the vertical joints are aligned perfectly.

Before building any higher, embed a wire reinforcing strip running from pier to pier in the next mortar bed (**3**). Continue to build the piers and screen up to a maximum height of 6 feet, inserting a wire strip into alternate courses. Finally, lay coping slabs at the top of each pier and along the top of the screen (**5**).

If you don't like the appearance of ordinary mortar joints, take out some of the mortar and repoint with mortar made with silver sand. A concave joint suits decorative screening (▷).

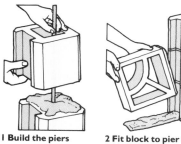

1 Build the piers   **2 Fit block to pier**   **3 Butter edge of block**

4 Lay a wire reinforcing strip into the mortar   **5 Lay coping slabs along the wall**

CAVITY WALLS

Cavity walls are used in the construction of buildings to prevent the passage of moisture through the wall to the interior. This is achieved by building two independent leaves of masonry with a clear gap between them. The gap provides a degree of thermal insulation but the insulation value increases appreciably if an efficient insulant is introduced to the cavity (▷). The exterior leaf of most cavity walls is constructed with facing bricks. The inner leaf is sometimes built with interior-grade bricks but more often with concrete blocks. Whatever type of masonry is used, both leaves must be tied together with wall ties spanning the gap. Cavity walls are likely to be load-bearing, and so have to be built very accurately—hire a professional to construct them. Make sure the bricklayer includes a DPC in both leaves and avoids dropping mortar into the gap. If mortar collects at the base of the cavity, or even on one of the wall ties, moisture can bridge the gap leading to dampness on the inside.

Cavity wall construction
A section through a typical cavity wall built with an exterior leaf of bricks tied to an inner leaf of plastered concrete blocks.

Building a brick base and piers
Build piers and a low base of bricks or facing blocks (▷), including reinforcing bars in the center of each pier. Lay coping slabs along the wall and continue to build the piers along with the screen. Tie the screen and piers together with reinforcing strips as described at left, but insert standard wall ties in alternate courses to provide additional location and support.

R-VALUES FOR COMMON INSULATION MATERIALS

Material	Approx. R-Value (per inch)
Fiberglass	3.5
Mineral fiber	3.5
Cellulose	3.7
Polystyrene (beadboard)	4.0
Polystyrene (extruded)	5.0
Polyurethane	7.0
Isocyanurate	7.5

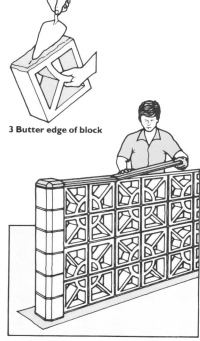

BUILDING WITH STONE

Constructing garden walls with natural stone requires a different approach than that needed for bricklaying or building with concrete blocks. A stone wall must be as stable as one built with any other masonry material, but its visual appeal relies on less regular coursing. In fact, there is no real coursing at all in the usual sense when the wall is built with undressed stone or rubble.

Structural considerations

Stone walls don't necessarily require mortar to hold the stones together, although it is often used, especially with dressed or semidressed stone, to provide additional stability. As a result, many stone walls taper, having a wide base of heavy, flat stones and gradually decreasing in width as the wall rises.

This traditional form of construction developed to prevent a wall of unmortared stones from toppling sideways under the pressure of high winds or animals. Far from detracting from its appearance, the inherent informality of natural stone walling suits a country-style garden perfectly.

Building a dry-stone wall

A true dry-stone wall is built without mortar, relying instead on a selective choice of stones and careful placement to provide stability. Experience is needed for perfect results, but there is no reason why you cannot introduce mortar, particularly within the core of the wall, and still maintain the appearance of dry-stone construction. You can also bed the stones in soil, packing it firmly into the crevices as you lay each course. This enables you to plant ferns or other suitable plants in the wall, even during construction.

When you select the masonry, look out for flat stones in a variety of sizes, and make sure you have some large enough to run the full width of the wall, especially at the base of the structure. These bonding stones, placed at regular intervals, are important components which tie the loose rubble into a cohesive structure. Even a low wall will inevitably include some heavy stones. When you lift them, keep your back straight and your feet together, using the strong muscles of your legs to take the strain.

DESIGNING THE WALL

Every dry-stone wall must be "battered." In other words, it must have a wide base and sides that slope inward. For a wall about 3 feet in height (and it is risky to build a dry-stone wall any higher) the base should be no less than 18 inches wide. You should aim to provide a minimum slope of 1 inch for every 2 feet of height.

Traditionally, the base of this type of wall rests on a 4-inch bed of sand laid on a compacted soil at the bottom of a shallow trench. For a more reliable foundation, lay a 4-inch concrete footing (◁), making it about 4 inches wider than the wall on each side.

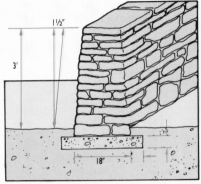

Proportions of a stone-built wall

Constructing the wall

Assuming you are using soil as a jointing material, spread a 1-inch layer over the footing and place a substantial bonding stone across the width to form the bed of the first course (1). Lay other stones about the same height as the bonding stone along each side of the wall, pressing them down into the soil to make a firm base. It is worth stretching a builder's line (◁) along each side of the wall to help you make a reasonably straight base.

Lay smaller stones between to fill out the base of the wall (2), then pack more soil into all the crevices.

Spread another layer of soil on top of the base and lay a second course of stones, bridging the joints between the stones below (3). Press them down so that they angle inwards towards the center of the wall. Check by eye that the coursing is about level as you build the wall and remember to include bonding stones at regular intervals.

Introduce plants into the larger crevices or hammer smaller stones into the chinks to lock the large stones in place (4).

At the top of the wall, either fill the core with soil for plants or lay large, flat coping stones, firming them with packed soil. Finally, brush loose soil from the faces of the wall.

1 Lay a bonding stone at the end of the wall

2 Fill out the base with small stones

3 Lay a second course of stones

4 Fill the chinks

BUILDING RETAINING WALLS

Retaining walls hold back a bank of earth. But don't attempt to cut into a steep bank and restrain it with a single high wall. Apart from the obvious danger of the wall collapsing, terracing the slope with a series of low walls is a more attractive solution which offers opportunities for imaginative planting.

Choosing your materials

Bricks and concrete blocks are perfectly suitable materials to choose for constructing a retaining wall, providing they are built sturdily. It is best to support these walls with reinforcing bars buried in the concrete footing (▷). Run the bars through hollow-core blocks (**1**) or build a double skin of brickwork, rather like a miniature cavity wall, using wall ties to bind each skin together (**2**).

The mass and weight of natural stone make it ideal for retaining walls. The wall should be battered to an angle of 2 inches to every foot of height so that it virtually leans into the bank (**3**). Keep the height below 3 feet for safety.

A skillful builder could construct a dry-stone retaining wall perfectly safely, but use mortar for additional ridigity and support if you are an amateur.

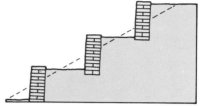

Terracing with retaining walls

1 A retaining wall of hollow concrete blocks

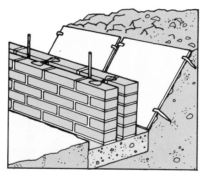

2 Use two skins of brick tied together

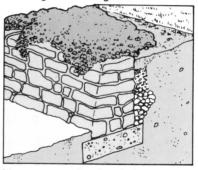

3 Lean a stone wall against the bank of earth

Constructing a stone wall

Excavate the soil to provide enough room to dig the footing (▷) and construct the wall. If the soil is loosely packed, restrain it temporarily with sheets of scrap plywood, corrugated iron or similar sheeting. Drive long metal pegs into the bank to hold the sheets in place (**1**). Lay the footing at the base of the bank and allow it to set before building the wall.

Lay uncut stones as if you were building a dry-stone wall (▷), but set each course on mortar. If you use regular stone blocks, select stones of different proportions to add interest to the wall, and stagger the joints. Use standard bricklaying methods (▷) to bed the stones in mortar.

It is essential to allow for drainage behind the wall to prevent the soil's becoming waterlogged. When you lay the second course of stones, embed ¾-inch plastic pipes in the mortar bed, allowing them to slope slightly toward the front of the wall. The pipes should be placed at about 3-foot intervals and pass right through the wall, projecting a little from the face (**2**).

FINISHING STONE WALLS

When the wall is complete, rake out the joints to give a dry-wall appearance. An old paintbrush is a useful tool for smoothing the mortar in deep crevices to make firm, watertight joints. Alternatively, point regular stones as for brickwork (▷).

Allow the mortar to set for a day or two before filling behind the wall. Lay gravel at the base to cover the drainage pipes to help reduce the force of groundwater pressure. Provide a generous layer of topsoil so that you can plant up to the wall.

1 Hold back the earth with scrap boards

2 Set plastic pipes in the wall for drainage

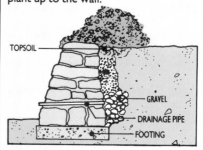

TOPSOIL
GRAVEL
DRAINAGE PIPE
FOOTING

Filling behind a stone wall

PATHS, DRIVES AND PATIOS

For many people, paving of any kind is associated with an unpleasant urban environment, conjuring up an image of a concrete patch devoid of plants, trees and grass—inhuman and unattractive. In reality, introducing paving to a garden provides an opportunity to create surprising contrasts of color and texture intensified by sunlight and deep shadows. The harshness of a hard, unyielding surface is softened by the addition of foliage, while certain sculptural plants which recede into a background of soil and grass are seen to advantage against stone and gravel.

A paved patio
A paved area surrounded by stone or brick walls makes a perfect suntrap for swimming and relaxing.

Designing paved areas
The marriage of different materials offers numerous possibilities. It may be convenient to define areas of paving as paths, drives and patios, but they are only names to describe the function of those particular spaces in the garden. There is no reason why you cannot blend one area into another using the same material throughout, or use similar colors to link one type of paving with another. On the other hand, you could take a completely different approach and deliberately juxtapose coarse and smooth textures, or use pale and dark tones to make one space stand out from the next.

Having so many choices at your disposal does have its drawbacks. There is a strong temptation to experiment with any and every combination until the end result is a distracting mishmash. A few well-chosen materials which complement the house and its surroundings produce an environment which is not only more appealing in the short term, but actually improves as the garden matures.

Working with concrete

Concrete might not be everybody's first choice for paving a garden, but it is such a versatile material that you may not even be aware of its use. When it is cast into paving slabs (◁), for instance, it can be mistaken for natural stone, or you might be more aware of the geometric pattern created by the combination of individual units rather than the material itself. Even ordinary concrete can be finished with a surprising variety of textures, and is incomparable as a material for the foundations of outbuildings or extensions.

THE INGREDIENTS OF CONCRETE

Concrete in its simplest form consists of cement and fine particles of stone—sand and pebbles—known as aggregate. The dry ingredients are mixed with water to create a chemical reaction with the cement which binds the aggregate into a hard, dense material. The initial hardening process takes place quite quickly. The mix becomes unworkable after a couple of hours, depending on the temperature and humidity, but the concrete has no real strength for three to seven days. The process continues for up to a month, or as long as there is moisture present within the concrete. Moisture is essential to the reaction and the concrete must not dry out too quickly in the first few days.

CEMENT

Standard portland cement, sold in 94-pound bags from builders' supplies or DIY outlets, is used in the manufacture of concrete. In its dry condition, it is a fine, gray powder.

SAND

Sharp sand, a rather coarse and gritty material, constitutes part of the aggregate of a concrete mix. Don't buy fine builders' sand used for mortar, and avoid unwashed or beach sand, both of which contain impurities that could affect the quality of the concrete. Sharp sand is sold by the cubic yard from a builders' supply, although it is perhaps more convenient to buy it in large plastic bags if you have to transport it by car or van.

COARSE AGGREGATE

Coarse aggregate is gravel or crushed stone composed of particles large enough to be retained by a ¼-inch sieve up to a maximum size of ¾ inch for normal use. Once again, it can be bought loose by the cubic yard or in smaller quantities packed in plastic sacks.

PIGMENTS

Special pigments can be added to concrete, but it is difficult to guarantee an even color from one batch of concrete to another.

COMBINED AGGREGATE

Naturally occurring sand and gravel mix, known as ballast, is sold as a combined aggregate for concrete. The proportion of sand to gravel is not guaranteed unless the ballast has been reconstituted to adjust the mix, and you may have to do it yourself. In any case, make sure it has been washed to remove impurities.

DRY-MIXED CONCRETE

You can buy dry cement, sand and aggregate mixed to the required proportions for making concrete. Choose the proportion that best suits the job you have in mind (◁). Concrete mix is sold in various size bags up to 100 pounds. Available from the usual outlets, it is a more expensive way of buying the ingredients, but is a simple and convenient method of ordering exactly the amount you will need. Before you add water to the mix, make sure the ingredients are mixed thoroughly.

WATER

Use ordinary tap water to mix concrete, never river or sea water.

PVA ADDITIVES

You can buy PVA additives from builders' suppliers to make a smoother concrete mix which is less susceptible to frost damage.

MIXING CONCRETE

You can rent small mixing machines if you have to prepare a large volume of concrete, but for the average job it is just as convenient to mix concrete by hand. It isn't necessary to weigh out the ingredients when mixing concrete. Simply mix them by volume, choosing the proportions that suit the job at hand.

Mixing by hand

Use large buckets to measure the ingredients, one for the cement and an identical one for the aggregate, in order to keep the cement perfectly dry. Different shovels are also a good idea. Measure the materials accurately, leveling them with the rim of the bucket. Tap the side of the bucket with the shovel as you load it with sand or cement to shake down the loose particles.

Mix the sand and aggregate first on a hard, flat surface. Scoop a depression in the pile for the measure of cement, and mix all the ingredients until they form an even color.

Form another depression and add some water from a watering can. Push the dry ingredients into the water from around the edge until surface water is absorbed, then mix the batch by chopping the concrete with the shovel (1). Add more water, turning concrete from the bottom of the pile, and chop it as before until the whole batch has an even consistency. To test the workability of the mix, form a series of ridges by dragging the back of the shovel across the pile (2). The surface of the concrete should be flat and even in texture, and the ridges should hold their shape without slumping.

1 Mixing ingredients
Mix the ingredients by chopping the concrete mix with the shovel. Turn the mix over and chop again.

2 Testing the mix
Make ridges with the back of the shovel to test the workability of the mix.

Mixing by machine

Make sure you set up the concrete mixer on a hard, level surface and that the drum is upright before you start the motor. Use a bucket to pour half the measure of coarse aggregate into the drum and add water. This will clean the drum after each batch has been mixed. Add the sand and cement alternately in small batches, plus the rest of the aggregate. Add water little by little along with the other ingredients.

Let the batch mix for a few minutes. Then, with the drum of the mixer still rotating, turn out a little concrete into a wheelbarrow to test its consistency (see above). If necessary, return the concrete to the mixer to adjust it.

Storing materials

If you buy sand and coarse aggregate in sacks, simply use whatever you need at a time, keeping the rest bagged up until required. If you buy the materials loose, store them in piles, separated by a wooden plank if necessary, on a hard surface or thick polyethylene sheets. Protect the materials from prolonged rain with weighted sheets of plastic.

Storing cement is more critical. It is sold in paper sacks which will absorb moisture from the ground, so pile them on a board propped up on spacers. Keep cement in a dry shed or garage if possible, but if you have to store it outdoors, cover the bags with sheets of plastic weighted down with bricks. Once open, cement can absorb moisture from the air. Keep a partly used bag in a sealed plastic sack.

MACHINE SAFETY

- Make sure you understand the operating instructions before turning on the machine.
- Prop the mixer level and stable with blocks of wood.
- Never put your hands or shovel into the drum while the mixer is running.
- Don't lean over a rotating drum when you inspect the contents. It is good practice to wear goggles when mixing concrete.

READY-MIXED CONCRETE

If you need a lot of concrete for a driveway or large patio it may be worth ordering a supply of ready-mixed concrete from a local supplier. Always speak to the supplier well before you need the concrete to discuss your particular requirements. Specify the proportions of the ingredients and say whether you will require the addition of a retarding agent to slow down the setting time. Once a normal mix of concrete is delivered, you will have no more than two hours to finish the job. A retarding agent can add up to two hours to the setting time. Tell the supplier what you need the concrete for and accept his advice.

For quantities of less than 6 cubic yards you might have to shop around for a supplier who is willing to deliver without an additional charge. Discuss any problems of discharging the concrete on site. To avoid transporting the concrete too far by wheelbarrow, have it discharged as close to the site as possible, if not directly into place. The chute on a delivery truck can reach only so far, and if the truck is too large or heavy to drive onto your property you will need several helpers to move the quantity of concrete while it is still workable. A single cubic yard of concrete will fill 25 to 30 large wheelbarrows. If it takes longer than 30 to 40 minutes to discharge the load, you may have to pay extra.

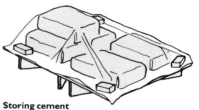

Storing sand and aggregate
Separate the piles of sand and aggregate with a wooden plank.

Storing cement
Raise bags of cement off the ground and cover them with plastic sheeting.

● **Professional mixing**
There are companies who will deliver concrete ingredients and mix them to your specification on the spot. All you have to do is transport the concrete and pour it into place. There is no waste as you only pay for the concrete you use. Telephone a local company for details on price and minimum quantity.

DESIGNING CONCRETE PAVING

The idea of having to design simple concrete pads and pathways might seem odd, but there are important factors to consider if the concrete is to be durable. At the least, you will have to decide on the thickness of the concrete to support the weight of traffic, and determine the angle of slope required to drain off surface water. When the area of concrete is large or a complicated shape, you must incorporate control joints to allow the material to expand and contract without cracking. If a pad is for a habitable building, it must include a damp-proof membrane to prevent moisture from rising from the ground (◁). Even the proportions of sand, cement and aggregate used must be considered carefully to suit the function of the paving.

Deciding on the slope

In theory, a free-standing pad can be laid perfectly level, especially when it is supporting a small outbuilding, but, in fact, a very slight slope or fall prevents water from collecting in puddles if you have failed to get the concrete absolutely flat. When a pad is laid directly against a house, it must have a definite fall away from the building, and any parking area or drive must shed water to provide adequate traction for vehicles and to minimize the formation of ice. When concrete is laid against a building, it must be at least 6 inches below the existing damp-proof course.

USE OF PAVING	ANGLE OF FALL
Pathways	Not required
Drive	1 in 40 1 in. per yard
Patio Parking area	1 in 60 away from building 1 in. per yard
Outbuildings	1 in 80 toward the door ½ in. per yard

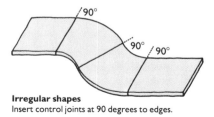

Irregular shapes
Insert control joints at 90 degrees to edges.

RECOMMENDED THICKNESSES FOR CONCRETE

The natural thicknesses recommended for concrete paving assumes it will be laid on a firm subsoil, but if the soil is clay or peat, increase the thickness by about 50 percent. The same applies to a new site where the soil might not be compacted. Unless the concrete is for pedestrian traffic only, lay a subbase of compacted gravel below the paving. This will absorb ground movement without affecting the concrete itself. A subbase is not essential for a very lightweight structure like a small wooden shed, but since you might want to increase the weight at some time, it is wise to install a subbase at the outset.

PATHWAYS

For pedestrian traffic only
Concrete: 4 in.
Subbase: Not needed

PATIOS

Any extensive area of concrete for pedestrian traffic
Concrete: 4 to 6 in.
Subbase: 4 in.

DRIVEWAYS

A drive which is used for an average family car only
Concrete: 4 in.
Subbase: 4 in.
For heavier vehicles like delivery trucks
Concrete: 6 in.
Subbase: 4 in.

LIGHT STRUCTURES

A support pad for a wooden shed, green-house, and the like
Concrete: 4 in.
Subbase: 3 in.

PARKING SPACES

Exposed paving for parking the family car
Concrete: 4 in.
Subbase: 4 in.

GARAGES

Thicken up the edges of a garage pad to support the weight of the walls
Concrete:
Floor: 4 in.
Edges: 8 in.
Subbase:
Minimum 4 in.

Allowing for expansion

Changes in temperature cause concrete to expand and contract. If this movement is allowed to happen at random, a pad or pathway will crack at the weakest or most vulnerable point. A control joint, composed of a compressible material (◁), will absorb the movement or concentrate the force in predetermined areas where it does little harm. Joints should meet the sides of a concrete area at more or less 90 degrees. Always place a control joint between concrete and a wall, and around inspection chambers.

Positioning control joints

The position of control joints depends on the area and shape of the concrete.

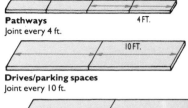

Pathways   4 FT.
Joint every 4 ft.

Drives/parking spaces   10 FT.
Joint every 10 ft.

Concrete slabs   10 FT.
Joints no more than 10 ft. apart and around drains

Divide a pad into equal bays if:
● Length is more than twice the width.
● Longest dimension is more than 40 × thickness.
● Longest dimension exceeds 10 ft.

CALCULATING QUANTITIES OF CONCRETE

Estimate the amount of materials you require by calculating the volume of concrete in the finished pad, path or drive.

Measure the surface area of the site and multiply that figure by the thickness of the concrete.

Estimating quantities of concrete

Use the gridded diagram to estimate the volume of concrete by reading off the area of the site in square yards and tracing it across horizontally to meet the angled line indicating the thickness of the concrete. Trace the line up to find the volume of concrete needed for your job in cubic yards.

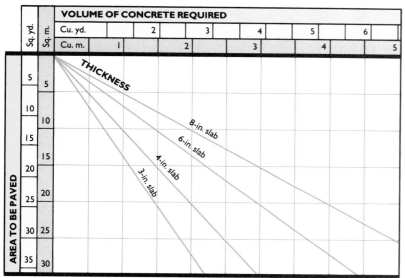

Estimating quantities of ingredients

Use the bar charts to estimate how much cement, sand and aggregate is needed to mix up the volume of concrete worked out by using the chart above.

The figures are based on the amount of ingredients used to mix one cubic yard of concrete using a particular type of mix (see below) plus about 10 percent for waste.

CALCULATING AREA

Squares and rectangles
Calculate the area of rectangular paving by multiplying width by length:

Example:
2 ft. × 3 ft. = 6 sq. ft.
78 in. × 117 in. = 9126 sq. in. or 7 sq. yds.

Circles
Use the formula πr^2 to calculate the area of a circle. $\pi = 3.14$. r = radius of circle.

Example:
3.14×2 ft.$^2 = 3.14 \times 4 = 12.56$ sq. ft.
3.14×78 in.$^2 = 3.14 \times 6084 = 19,104$ sq. in. or 14.75 sq. yds.

Irregular shapes
Draw an irregular area of paving on graph paper. Count the whole squares and average out the portions to find the approximate area.

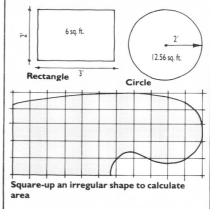

Square-up an irregular shape to calculate area

SEE ALSO
Details for: ▷
Mixing concrete   41

	CUBIC YARDS OF CONCRETE								
	1.00	1.50	2.00	2.50	3.00	3.50	4.00	4.50	5.00
GENERAL-PURPOSE MIX									
Cement (94-lb. bags)	3.50	5.25	7.00	8.25	10.50	12.25	14.00	15.75	17.50
Sand (Cu. yds.)	0.50	0.75	1.00	1.25	1.50	1.75	2.00	2.25	2.50
Aggregate (Cu. yds.)	0.75	1.15	1.50	1.90	2.25	2.65	3.00	3.40	3.75
Ballast (Cu. yds.)	0.90	1.35	1.80	2.25	2.70	3.15	3.60	4.05	4.50
FOUNDATION MIX									
Cement (94-lb. bags)	3.00	4.50	6.00	7.50	9.00	10.50	12.00	13.50	15.00
Sand (Cu. yds.)	0.55	0.80	1.10	1.40	1.65	1.95	2.20	2.50	2.75
Aggregate (Cu. yds.)	0.75	1.15	1.50	1.90	2.25	2.65	3.00	3.40	3.75
Ballast (Cu. yds.)	1.00	1.50	2.00	2.50	3.00	3.50	4.00	4.50	5.00
PAVING MIX									
Cement (94-lb. bags)	9.00	13.50	18.00	22.50	27.00	31.50	36.00	40.50	45.00
Sand (Cu. yds.)	0.45	0.70	0.90	1.15	1.35	1.60	1.80	2.00	2.25
Aggregate (Cu. yds.)	0.75	1.15	1.50	1.90	2.25	2.65	3.00	3.40	3.75
Ballast (Cu. yds.)	1.00	1.50	2.00	2.50	3.00	3.50	4.00	4.50	5.00

CLEANING TOOLS AND MACHINERY

Keep the shovel as clean as possible between mixing batches of concrete, and at the end of a working day wash all traces of concrete from your tools and wheelbarrow.

When you have finished using a concrete mixer, add a few shovels of coarse aggregate and a little water, then run the machine for a couple of minutes to scour the inside of the drum. Dump the aggregate, then hose out the drum with clean water.

Shovel unused concrete into sacks ready for disposal at a refuse dump and wash the mixing area with a stiff broom. Never hose concrete or any of the separate ingredients into a drain.

POURING A CONCRETE SLAB

Laying a simple slab as a base for a small shed or similar structure involves all the basic principles of concrete work: building a retaining formwork, as well as the pouring, leveling and finishing of concrete. As long as the base is less than 6 square feet, there is no need to include control joints.

Mixing concrete by volume

Mixing the ingredients by volume is the easiest and most accurate way to guarantee the required proportions. Whatever container you use to measure the ingredients of concrete—shovel, bucket or wheelbarrow —the proportions remain the same.

MIXING CONCRETE BY VOLUME		
Type of mix	Proportions	For 1 cu. yd. concrete
GENERAL PURPOSE		
Use in most situations including covered pads other than garage floors	1 part cement	3 bags (94-lb.)
	2 parts sand	0.5 cu. yd.
	3 parts aggregate	0.7 cu. yd.
	4 parts ballast	0.9 cu. yd.
FOUNDATION		
Use for footings at the base of masonry walls	1 part cement	2.5 bags (94-lb.)
	2½ parts sand	0.5 cu. yd.
	3½ parts aggregate	0.7 cu. yd.
	5 parts ballast	1.0 cu. yd.
PAVING		
Use for exposed pads such as drives, parking areas or footpaths, but also for garage floors	1 part cement	4 bags (94-lb.)
	1½ parts sand	0.5 cu. yd.
	2½ parts aggregate	0.7 cu. yd.
	3½ parts ballast	1.0 cu. yd.

Excavating the site

Mark out the area of the pad with string lines attached to pegs driven into the ground outside the work area (**1**). Remove them to excavate the site but replace them later to help position the formwork which will hold the concrete in place.

Remove the topsoil and all vegetation within the excavation site down to a level which allows for the combined thickness of concrete and subbase. Extend the area of excavation about 6 inches outside the space marked out for the pad. Cut back any roots you encounter. Put the turf aside to cover the infill surrounding the completed pad. Level the bottom of the excavation by dragging a board across it (**2**), and compact the soil with a garden roller.

Erecting the formwork

Until the concrete sets hard, it must be supported all around by formwork. For a straightforward rectangular slab, construct the formwork from 1-inch-thick wood planks set on edge. The planks, which must be as wide as the finished depth of concrete, are held in place temporarily with stout 2 × 2-inch wooden stakes. Secondhand or form-grade lumber is quite adequate. If it is slightly thinner than an inch, just use more stakes to brace it. If you have to join planks, butt them end to end, nailing a cleat on the outside (**3**).

Using the string lines as a guide, erect one board at the higher end of the pad, and drive stakes behind it at about 3-foot intervals or less, with one for each corner. The tops of the stakes and board must be level and correspond exactly to the proposed surface of the pad. Nail the board to the stakes (**4**).

Set up another board opposite, but before you nail it to the stakes, establish the crossfall (◁) with a straightedge and level. Work out the difference in level from one end of the pad to the other. For example, a pad which is 6 feet long should drop an inch over that distance. Tape a shim to one end of the straightedge, and with the shim resting on the low stakes, place the other end on the opposite board (**5**). Drive home each low stake until the level reads horizontal. Then nail the board flush with the tops of the stakes.

Erect the sides of the formwork, allowing the ends of the boards to overshoot the corners to make it easier to dismantle them when the concrete has set (**6**). Use the straightedge, this time without the shim, to level the boards across the formwork.

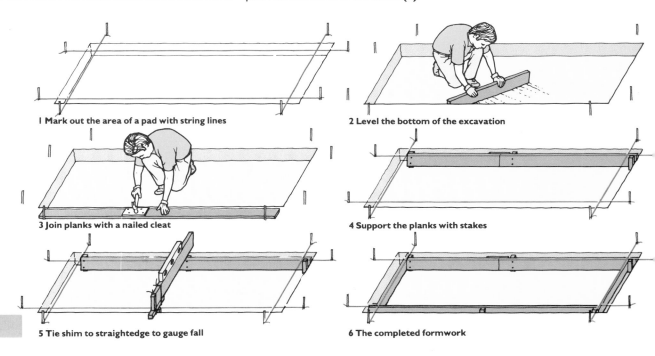

1 Mark out the area of a pad with string lines

2 Level the bottom of the excavation

3 Join planks with a nailed cleat

4 Support the planks with stakes

5 Tie shim to straightedge to gauge fall

6 The completed formwork

POURING A CONCRETE SLAB

Laying the subbase

A mixture of gravel and sand is an ideal material for a subbase, but you can use crushed stone or brick as long as you throw out any plaster, scrap metal or similar rubbish. Also remove large lumps of masonry as they will not compact well. Pour gravel into the formwork and rake it fairly level before tamping it down with a heavy length of wood (7). Break up any stubborn lumps with a heavy hammer. Fill in low spots with more gravel or sharp sand until the subbase comes up to the underside of the formwork boards.

Filling with concrete

Mix the concrete as near to the site as is practicable and transport the fresh mix to the formwork in a wheelbarrow. Set up firm runways of scaffold boards if the ground is soft, especially around the perimeter of the formwork. Dampen the subbase and formwork with a fine spray and let surface water evaporate before tipping the concrete in place. Start filling from one end of the site and push the concrete firmly into the corners (8). Rake it level until the concrete stands about ¾ inch above the level of the boards.

Tamp down the concrete with the edge of a 2-inch-thick plank long enough to span across the formwork. Starting at one end of the site, compact the concrete with steady blows of the plank, moving it along by about half its thickness each time (9). Cover the whole area twice, then remove excess concrete using the plank with a sawing action (10). Fill any low spots, then compact and level once more.

Cover the pad with sheets of polyethylene, taped at the joints to retain the moisture and weighted down with bricks around the edge (11). Alternatively, use wet burlap which you must keep damp for three days using a fine spray. Try to avoid pouring concrete in very cold weather, but if it is unavoidable, spread a layer of earth or sand on top of the sheeting to insulate the concrete from frost. You can walk on the concrete after three days, but leave it for about a week before removing the formwork and erecting a shed or similar outbuilding on it.

SEE ALSO

Details for: ▷

Mixing concrete	41
Control joints	46

Extending a slab
If you want to enlarge a patio, simply butt a new section of concrete against the existing slab. The butt joint will form a control joint. To add a narrow strip, for a larger shed for instance, drill holes in the edge of the pad and use epoxy adhesive to glue in short reinforcing rods before pouring the fresh concrete.

Finishing the edges
If any of the edges are exposed, the sharp corners might cause a painful injury. Round the corners with a homemade edging float. Bend a piece of sheet metal over a ¾-in.-diameter rod or tube and screw a handle in the center. Run the float along the formwork as you finish the surface of the concrete.

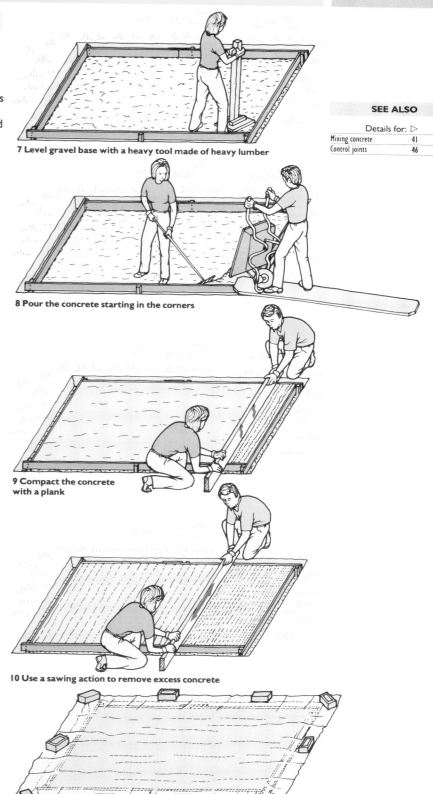

7 Level gravel base with a heavy tool made of heavy lumber

8 Pour the concrete starting in the corners

9 Compact the concrete with a plank

10 Use a sawing action to remove excess concrete

11 Cover the pad with weighted sheets of plastic

POURING PATHS AND DRIVES

Paths and drives are poured and compacted in the same way as simple rectangular slabs, using similar framework to contain the fresh concrete. But the proportions of most paths and drives necessitate the inclusion of control joints to allow for expansion and contraction (◁). You must install a subbase beneath a drive, but a footpath can be poured on compacted soil leveled with sharp sand. Establish a slight fall across the site to shed rainwater (◁). Don't use a vehicle on concrete for 10 days after laying.

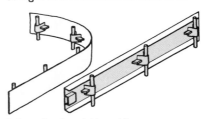

1 A water level made from a garden hose

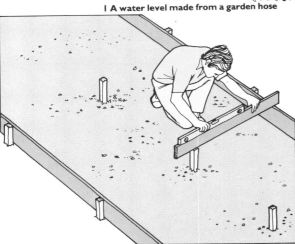

2 Level formwork using a reference stake

DRAIN

A sloping drive

If you build a drive on a sloping site, make the transition from level ground as gentle as possible. If it runs toward a garage, let the last 6 ft. slope up toward the door. Use a pole to impress a drain across the wet concrete at the lowest point.

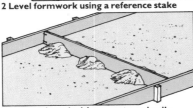

5 Support board with concrete and nails

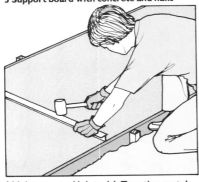

6 Make a control joint with T-section metal

Setting out paths and drives

Excavate the site, allowing for the thickness of subbase and concrete. Level the bottom of the excavation as accurately as you can, using a board to scrape the surface flat.

Drive accurately leveled pegs into the ground along the site to act as datum points for the formwork. Space them about 6 feet apart down the center of the pathway. Drive in the first peg until its top corresponds exactly to the proposed surface of the concrete. Use a long straightedge and level to position every other peg or, better still, use a homemade water level. Push a short length of transparent plastic tubing into each end of an ordinary garden hose. Fill the hose with water until it appears in the tube at both ends. As long as the ends remain open, the water level at each end is constant so that you can establish a level over any distance, even around obstacles or corners. Tie one end of the hose to the first reference stake so that the water level aligns with the top of the peg. Use the other to establish the level of every other peg along the pathway (**1**). Cork each end of the hose to retain the water as you move it.

To set a fall with a water level, make a mark on one tube below the surface of the water and use that as a gauge for the top of the peg.

Erecting formwork

Construct formwork from 1-inch-thick planks as for a concrete slab (◁). To check that it is level, rest a straightedge on the nearest reference stake (**2**).

If the drive or path is very long, wood formwork can be expensive. It might be cheaper to rent metal road forms (**3**). Straight-sided formwork is made from rigid units, but flexible sections are available to form curves.

If you want to bend wooden formwork, make a series of parallel saw cuts across the width of the plank in the area of the curve (**4**). The wood is less likely to snap if you place the saw cuts on the inside of the bend.

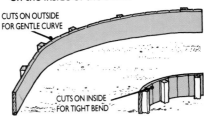

CUTS ON OUTSIDE FOR GENTLE CURVE

CUTS ON INSIDE FOR TIGHT BEND

3 Curved and straight road forms

4 Curved formwork made with wooden planks

Installing control joints

Install a permanent expansion joint every 4 feet for a footpath and every 10 feet along a drive. Cut strips of treated hardboard or ¾-inch-thick softwood to fit exactly between the formwork and to match the depth of the concrete. Before pouring, hold the control joints in place with mounds of concrete and nails on each side of the board driven into the formwork (**5**). Pack more concrete carefully on each side of the joints as you fill the formwork and tamp toward them from both sides so that they are not dislodged.

As the joints are permanent fixtures, make sure they are level with the surface of the concrete. Install similar joints in a patio or use an alternate-bay construction (see opposite page).

To prevent concrete from cracking between joints on a narrow path, cut ¾-inch-deep grooves across the compacted concrete to form dummy joints alternating with the actual ones. The simplest method is to cut a length of T-section metal to fit between the formwork boards. Place it on the surface of the wet concrete and tap it down with a mallet (**6**). Carefully lift the strip out of the concrete to leave a neat impression. If the concrete should move, a crack will develop unnoticed at the bottom of the groove.

Place strips of thick bituminous felt between concrete and an adjoining wall to absorb expansion. Hold the felt in place with mounds of concrete, as described at left, before pouring the full amount of concrete.

ALTERNATE-BAY METHOD OF CONSTRUCTION

It is not always possible to pour all the concrete in one operation. In such cases it is easier to divide the formwork crosswise with additional planks known as stop ends to form equal-size bays. By filling alternate bays with concrete, you have plenty of time to compact and level each section and more room in which to maneuver. It is a convenient way to pour a large patio which would be practically impossible to compact and level all at once, and it is the only method to use for drives or paths butting against a wall which makes it impossible to work across the width. Alternate-bay construction is often used for drives on a steep slope to prevent concrete from slumping downhill.

There is no need to install physical control joints as the simple butt joint between the bays is sufficient allowance for movement within the concrete.

Pouring concrete in alternate bays
Stand in the empty bays to compact concrete laid against a wall. When the first bays are set hard, remove the stop ends and fill the gaps, using the surface of the firm concrete as a level.

INSPECTION CHAMBERS

Prevent expansion from damaging grating by surrounding it with control joints. Place formwork around the chamber and fill with concrete. When set, remove the boards and place felt strips or treated wood boards on all sides.

Surround grating with formwork

SURFACE FINISHES FOR CONCRETE

The surface finishes produced by tamping or striking off with a sawing action are perfectly adequate for a skid-proof, workmanlike surface for a slab, drive or pathway, but you can produce a range of other finishes using simple hand tools once you have compacted and leveled the concrete.

Float finishes
Smooth the tamped concrete by sweeping the wooden float across the surface, or make an even finer texture by finishing with a trowel (steel float). Let the concrete dry out a little before using a float or you will bring water to the top and weaken it, eventually resulting in a dusty residue on the hardened concrete. Bridge the formwork with a stout plank so that you can reach the center, or rent a skip float with a long handle for large pads.

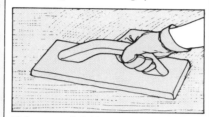

Make a smooth finish with a wooden float

Brush finishes
Make a finely textured surface by drawing a yard broom across the setting concrete. Flatten the concrete initially with a wooden float, them make parallel passes with the broom held at a low angle to avoid tearing the surface.

Texture the surface with a broom

Brush-finishing concrete

Exposed-aggregate finish
Embedding small stones or pebbles in the surface makes a very attractive and practical finish, but it takes a little practice to be successful.

Scatter dampened pebbles onto the freshly laid concrete and tamp them firmly with a length of timber until they are flush with the surface (**1**). Place a plank across the formwork and apply your full weight to make sure the surface is even. Let the concrete harden for a while until all surface water has evaporated, then use a very fine spray and a brush to wash away the cement from around the pebbles until they protrude (**2**). Cover the concrete for about 24 hours, then lightly wash the surface again to clean any sediment off the pebbles. Cover the concrete again and leave it to harden thoroughly.

1 Tamp pebbles into the fresh concrete

2 Wash the cement from around the pebbles

Exposed-aggregate finish

PRECAST PAVING UNITS

If your only experience with paving slabs is the rather bland variety used for public footpaths, then cast concrete paving may not seem a very attractive proposition for a garden. However, manufacturers can supply products in a wide range of shapes, colors and finishes that are sure to please.

Colors and textures

Paving units are made by hydraulic pressing or casting in molds to create the desired surface finish. Pigments and selected aggregates added to the concrete mix create the illusion of natural stone or a range of muted colors. Combining two or more colors within the same area of paving can be very striking.

1 Cobbles or sets
Large units resemble an area of smaller cobbles or sets. Careful laying and filling are essential. Sets are patterned in straight rows or as curves.

2 Planter
Four planter stones laid in a square leave a circle for a tree or shrub.

3 Exposed aggregate
Crushed-stone aggregate has a very pleasing mottled appearance, either exposed to make a coarse gritstone texture or polished flat to resemble terrazzo.

4 Brushed finishes
A brush-filling unit, textured with parallel grooves as if a stiff broom had been dragged across the wet concrete, is practical and nonslip. Straight or swirling patterns are available.

5 Riven stone
The finish resembles that of natural stone. The best-quality units are cast from real stone originals in a wide variety of subtle textures. If the texture continues over the edge of the slabs, they can be used for steps and coping.

SHAPES AND SIZES

Although some manufacturers offer a wider choice than others, there is a fairly standard range of shapes and modular sizes. You can carry the largest slabs by yourself, but it is a good idea to have an assistant when maneuvering them carefully into place.

Square and rectangular
One size and shape make gridlike patterns or, staggered, create a bonded brickwork effect. Rectangular slabs can form a basketweave or herringbone pattern. Or, combine different sizes to create the impression of random paving.

Regular grid

Staggered slabs

Basketweave pattern

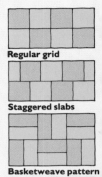

Herringbone pattern

Random paving

Hexagonal
Hexagonal slabs form honeycomb patterns. Use half slabs, running across flats or from point to point, to edge areas paved in straight lines.

Half-hexagonal slabs

Hexagonal slab

Honeycomb pattern

Tapered slabs
Use tapered slabs to edge ponds, or around trees, and for curved paths or steps. Lay them head to toe to make straight sections of paving. Use right- or left-hand half slabs at the ends.

Full and half-tapered slabs

Straight section

Circular
Circular slabs make perfect individual stepping stones across a lawn or flower bed, but for a wide area, fill the spaces between with cobbles or gravel.

Butted circular slabs

LAYING PAVING UNITS

Laying heavy paving units involves a fair amount of physical labor, but in terms of technique it is no more complicated than tiling a wall. Accurate setting out and careful laying, especially during the early stages, will produce perfect results. Take extra care when laying hexagonal units to ensure that the last of them fit properly.

CUTTING CONCRETE PAVING UNITS

Mark a line across a unit with a soft pencil or chalk. Then, using a bolster and hammer, chisel a groove about 1/8 inch deep following the line (**1**). Continue the groove down both edges and across the underside of the unit. Place the unit on a bed of sand and put a block of wood at one end of the groove. Strike the block with a hammer while moving it along the groove until a split develops through the slab (**2**). Clean up the rough edge with a bolster.

For a perfectly clean cut each time, hire an angle grinder fitted with a stone-cutting disc. Score a deep groove on both sides of the slab and across the edges. Tap along the groove with a bolster to propagate a crack.

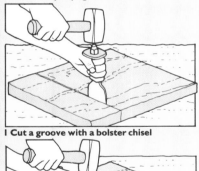

1 Cut a groove with a bolster chisel

2 Strike block over groove with a hammer

PROTECTING YOUR EYES

Whenever you cut masonry units with a chisel or a grinder, always protect your eyes from flying chips of concrete by wearing plastic goggles. An angle grinder throws up a lot of dust, so wear a simple gauze face mask as a safeguard.

Setting out the area of paving

Wherever possible, to eliminate the arduous task of cutting units to fit, plan an area of paving to be laid with whole slabs only. Use a straight wall as a reference line and measure away from it, or allow for a 4- to 6-inch margin of gravel between the paving and wall if the location dictates that you have to lay slabs toward the house. A gravel margin not only saves time and money by using fewer slabs, but also provides an area for planting climbers and adequate drainage to keep the wall dry. Even so, establish a 5/8-inch-per-yard slope across the paving so that most surface water will drain

Preparing a base for paving

Paving units must be laid upon a firm, level base, but the depth and substance of that base depends on the type of soil and the proposed use of the paving.

For straightforward patios and paths, remove vegetation and topsoil to allow for the thickness of the paving and a 1-inch layer of sharp sand. Set the paving about 3/4 inch below the level of surrounding turf to avoid damaging the lawn mower when you cut the grass. Having compacted the soil using a

into the garden. Any paving must be 6 inches below a damp-proof course to protect the building.

Since paving units are made to reasonably precise dimensions, marking out an area simply involves accurate measurement, allowing for a 1/4-inch gap between slabs. Some units are cast with sloping edges to provide a tapered joint (**1**) and should be butted edge to edge. Use stakes and string to mark out the perimeter of the paved area, and check your measurements before you excavate.

SEE ALSO

Details for : ▷	
Mixing mortar	27
Paving slope	42
Laying subbase	45

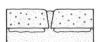

1 Tapered joint

garden roller, spread the sand with a rake and level it by scraping and tamping with a length of wood (**2**).

To support heavier loads, or if the soil is composed of clay or peat, lay a subbase (▷) of firmly compacted gravel—broken bricks or crushed stone—to a depth of 3 to 4 inches before spreading the sand to level the surface. If you plan to park vehicles on the paving, then increase the depth to 6 inches.

2 Level the sand base

Laying the paving slabs

Set up string lines again as a guide and lay the edging slabs on the sand, working in both directions from a corner. When you are satisfied with their positions, lift them one at a time and set them on a bed of mortar (1 part cement: 4 parts sand). Add just enough water to make a firm mortar. Lay a fist-size blob under each corner and one more to support the center of the slab (**3**). If you intend to drive vehicles across the paving, lay a continuous bed of mortar about 2 inches thick.

Lay three units at a time with 1/4-inch wooden spacers between them. Level each unit by tapping with a heavy hammer, using a block of wood (**4**).

Gauge the slope across the paving by setting up reference stakes along the high side (▷). Drive them into the ground until the top of each corresponds to the finished surface of the paving, then use the straightedge to check the fall on the slabs (**5**). Lay the remainder of the units, working out from the corner each time to keep the joints square. Remove the spacers before the mortar sets.

3 Lay blobs of mortar

4 Level the units

5 Check the fall with a level

Filling the joints

Don't walk on the paving for two to three days until the mortar has set. If you have to cross the area, lay planks across the slabs to spread the load.

To fill the gaps between the units, brush a dry mortar mix of 1 part cement: 3 parts sand into the open joints (**6**). Remove any surplus material from the surface of the paving, then sprinkle the area with a very fine spray of water to consolidate the mortar. Avoid dry mortaring if heavy rain is imminent; it may wash the mortar out.

6 Fill the joints

LAYING CRAZY PAVING

The informal nature of paths or patios laid with irregular-shaped paving stones has always been popular. The random jigsaw effect, which many people find more appealing than the geometric accuracy of neatly laid slabs, is also very easy to achieve. A good eye for shape and proportion is more important than a practiced technique.

Materials for crazy paving

You can use broken concrete slabs if you can find enough but, in terms of appearance, nothing compares with natural stone. Stratified rock which splits into thin layers of its own accord as it is quarried is ideal for crazy paving, and can be obtained at a very reasonable price if you can collect it yourself. Select stones which are approximately 1½ to 2 inches thick in a variety of shapes and sizes.

Crazy paving from broken concrete slabs

SETTING OUT AND LAYING A BASE

You can, if you wish, set out string lines to define straight edges to crazy paving, although they will never be as precisely defined as those formed with cast concrete slabs. Or, allow the stones to form a broken irregular junction with grass or shingle, perhaps setting one or two individual stones out from the edge of the paving to blend one area into the other.

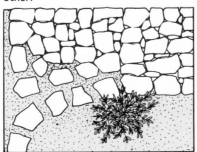

Create an irregular edge to crazy paving

Laying the stones

Arrange an area of stones, selecting them for a close fit but avoiding too many straight, continuous joints. Trim those that don't quite fit with a bolster and hammer. Reserve fairly large stones for the perimeter of the paved area, as small stones tend to break away.

Use a mallet or block of wood and a hammer to bed each stone into the sand (**1**) until they are all perfectly stable and reasonably level. Having bedded an area of about a square yard, use a straightedge and level to true up the stones (**2**). If necessary, add or remove sand beneath individual stones until the whole area is level. When the main area is complete, fill in the larger gaps with small stones, tapping them into place with a mallet (**3**).

Fill the joints by spreading more sand across the paving and sweeping it into the joints from all directions (**4**). Alternatively, mix up a stiff, almost dry, mortar and press it into the joints with a trowel, leaving no gaps.

Use an old paintbrush to smooth the mortared joints and wipe the stones clean with a damp sponge.

1 Bed the stones in the sand base

2 Check the level across several stones

3 Fill the gaps with small stones

4 Sweep dry sand into the joints

Laying stepping stones

Place individual stones or slabs across a lawn to form a row of stepping stones. Cut around the edge of each stone with a spade or trowel and remove the area of turf directly beneath. Scoop out the earth to allow for a one-inch bed of sharp sand plus the stone, which must be about ¾ inch below the level of the surrounding turf. Tap the stone into the sand until it no longer rocks when you step on it.

Cut around a stepping stone with a trowel

Stepping stones preserve a lawn

BRICK PATTERNS

Concrete bricks have one surface with chamfered edges all around, and spacers molded into the sides to form accurate joints. Common bricks can be laid on edge or face down showing the wide face normally unseen in a wall.

Unlike brick walls, which must be bonded in a certain way for stability (▷), brick paths can be laid in any pattern that appeals to you.

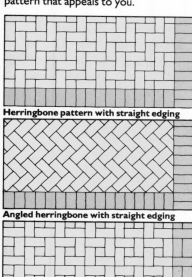

Herringbone pattern with straight edging

Angled herringbone with straight edging

Whole bricks surrounding colored half-bats

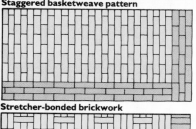

Staggered basketweave pattern

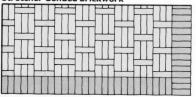

Stretcher-bonded brickwork

Cane-weave pattern

PAVING WITH BRICKS

Bricks make charming and attractive paths in a garden or lawn setting. The wide variety of textures and colors *available gives endless possibilities of pattern, bearing in mind the sort of use your paving can expect.*

Materials for brick paving

Common bricks are often selected for paths, and also small patios, even though there is the risk of spalling in freezing conditions unless they happen to be severe-weathering (SW) bricks (▷). The slightly uneven texture and color are the very reasons why secondhand bricks in particular are so much in demand for garden paving, so a little frost damage is usually acceptable.

Common bricks are not really suitable if the paved area is to be a parking space or drive, especially if it is to be used by heavy vehicles. For a durable surface, even under severe conditions, use modular bricks. They are slightly smaller than standard bricks, being $2\frac{1}{4} \times 3\frac{5}{8} \times 7\frac{5}{8}$ inches. Red or yellow are widely available and you can obtain other colors by special order.

Brick pavers
Clay brick pavers (top row) are made in a wide variety of colors and textures. *Concrete pavers* (bottom row) are less colorful but are available in more shapes.

Providing a base for brick paving

Lay brick footpaths and patios on a 3-inch gravel base (▷) covered with a 2-inch layer of sharp sand. To lay concrete bricks for a drive, increase the depth of gravel to 4 inches.

Fully compact the gravel and fill all voids that may have occurred so that

sand from the bedding course is not lost to the subbase.

Provide a cross-fall on patios and drives as for concrete (▷), and ensure that the surface of the paving is at least 6 inches below a damp-proof course to protect the building.

Retaining edges

Unless the brick path is laid against a wall or some similar structure, the edges of the paving must be contained by a permanent restraint. Lumber, treated with a chemical preservative, is one solution, constructed like the formwork for concrete (▷). The edging boards should be flush with the surface of the path, but drive the stakes below ground so that they can be covered by soil or turf (**1**).

As an alternative, set an edging of bricks in concrete (**2**). Dig a trench deep and wide enough to accommodate a row of bricks on end plus a 4-inch concrete foundation. Lay the bricks while the concrete is still wet, holding them in place temporarily with a staked board while you pack more concrete behind the edging. When the concrete has set, remove the board and lay gravel and sand in the excavation.

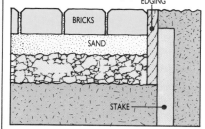

1 Wooden retaining edge

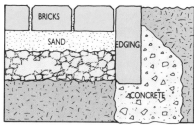

2 Brick retaining edge

LAYING THE BRICKS

Having chosen your bricks, prepared the ground and set retaining edges (▷), you can start laying your paving. When bricks are first laid upon the sand they should project ⅜ inch above the edging restraints to allow for bedding them in at a later stage (**1**). To level the sand for a path, cut a notched spreader to span the edging (**2**). If the paving is too wide for a spreader, lay leveling strips on the gravel base and scrape the sand to the required depth using a straightedge (**3**). Remove the strips and fill the voids carefully with sand. Keep the sand bed dry at all times. If it rains before you can lay the bricks, either let the sand dry out thoroughly or replace it with dry sand.

Lay an area of bricks on the sand to your chosen pattern. Work from one end of the site, kneeling on a board placed across the bricks (**4**). Never stand on the bed of sand. Lay whole bricks only, leaving any gaps at the edges to be filled with cut bricks after you

have laid an area of about a square yard. Concrete bricks have fixed spacers, so butt them together tightly.

Fill any remaining spaces with bricks cut with a bolster (◁). If you are paving a large area, you can rent an hydraulic guillotine (see left).

When the area of paving is complete, tamp the bricks into the sand bed by striking a 2 × 4 with a heavy sledgehammer. The 2 × 4 must be large enough to cover several bricks to maintain the level (**5**). For a really professional finish, rent a powered plate vibrator. Pass the vibrator over the paved area two or three times until it has worked the bricks down into the sand and flush with the outer edging (**6**). The act of vibrating bricks works sand up between them, but complete the job by brushing more sand across the finished paving and vibrate the sand into the open joints.

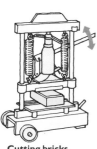

Cutting bricks
Rent an hydraulic brick-cutting guillotine to cut pavers.

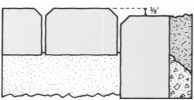

1 Start by laying bricks ⅜ in. above edging

2 Level the sand with a notched spreader

3 Or lay level battens on the gravel

4 Lay the bricks to your chosen pattern

5 Tamp the bricks with a hammer and 2 × 4

6 A vibrator levels brick paving perfectly

Plain concrete-brick drive and parking space

Mottled-brick garden path

Interlocking concrete pavers

Bricks laid to a herringbone pattern

COBBLESTONES AND GRAVEL

WOODEN PATHWAYS

Areas of cobblestones and gravel are used more for their decorative quality than as functional paving for drives or pathways. Cobbles, in particular, are most uncomfortable to walk on and, although a firmly consolidated area of gravel is fine for vehicles, walking on a gravel footpath can be rather like treading water. Both materials come into their own, however, when used as a foil for areas of flat paving slabs or bricks, and to set off plants such as dwarf conifers while keeping weed growth to a minimum.

Laying cobbles

Cobbles, large flint pebbles found on many a beach, can be laid loose, perhaps with larger rocks and plants. However, they are often set in mortar or concrete to create formal areas of texture.

Consolidate a layer of gravel (▷) and cover it with a leveled layer of dry concrete mix about 2 inches deep (▷).

Press the cobbles into the dry mix, packing them tightly together and projecting well above the surface. Use a 2 × 4 to tamp the area level (**1**). Then lightly sprinkle the whole area with water, both to set off the concrete hardening process and to clean the surfaces of the cobbles.

Large cobbles as a background to plants

Tamp the cobbles into a dry concrete mix

Laying gravel

If an area of gravel is to be used as a pathway or for motor vehicles, construct retaining edges of brick, concrete curbs or wooden boards as for brick paths (▷). This will stop gravel being spread outside its allotted area.

To construct a gravel drive, the subbase and the gravel itself must be compacted and leveled to prevent cars from skidding and churning up the material. Lay a 4-inch bed of firmed fill (▷) topped with 2 inches of very coarse gravel mixed with sand. Roll it flat. Rake a ¾- to 1-inch layer of fine pea gravel across the subbase and roll it down to make firm.

Making a gravel garden

To lay an area of gravel for planting, simply excavate the soil to accept a 1-inch-deep bed of fine gravel. Either set the gravel ¾ inch below the level of the lawn or edge the gravel garden with bricks or flat stones. Scrape away a small area of gravel for planting, then sprinkle it back again to cover the soil surrounding and right up to the plant itself.

COARSE GRAVEL
AND SAND
GRAVEL
PEA GRAVEL

Rake pea gravel across the surface of a drive

Gravel and conifer garden ▶

If you live in a rural district where large logs are plentiful or perhaps a mature tree has been felled in your garden, you can use 6-inch lengths of sawn logs set on end to make a practical and charming footpath. Either lay the logs together like crazy paving or use large individual pieces of wood as stepping stones. Hold wood rot at bay by soaking the sawn sections in buckets of chemical preservative.

Laying a log pathway

Excavate the area of the pathway to a depth of 8 inches and spread a 2-inch-deep layer of gravel and sand mix across the bottom. Use concreting ballast—combined aggregate—or make up the mix yourself (▷). Level the bed by scraping and tamping with a straightedge.

Place the logs on end on the bed, arranging them to create a pleasing combination of shapes and sizes (**1**). Work them into the sand until they stand firmly and evenly, then pour more sand and gravel between them (**2**). Brush the material across the pathway in all directions until the gaps between the logs are filled flush with the surface (**3**). If any logs stand proud so that they could cause someone to trip, tap them down with a heavy hammer.

If you want to plant between the logs, scrape out some sand and gravel and replace it with the appropriate soil.

1 Arrange the logs on end

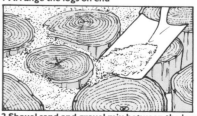

2 Shovel sand and gravel mix between the logs

3 Brush more mix into the joints

● **Use a heavy roller**
A lightweight garden roller is fine for compacting earth or sand, but use one weighing about 300 lbs. when leveling gravel.

- **Laying a new path**
Although cold cure tarmac is primarily a resurfacing material, it can be applied to a new gravel base as long as it is firmly compacted, leveled and sealed with a slightly more generous coat of bitumen emulsion.

- **Treating for heavy wear**
At entrance to drives and on bends, vehicle tires cause more wear than normal. Treat these areas with ¾-inch rolled layer of cold cure tarmac (see far right) before applying a dressing of stone chippings.

- **Double dressing**
If the surface you are dressing is in very poor condition or exceptionally loose, apply a first coat of bitumen emulsion at 7.25 lbs. per sq. yd. Cover with chippings and roll thoroughly. Two days later, sweep away loose chippings and apply a second coat of emulsion at 3.5 lbs. per sq. yd. and finish with chippings as described at right.

DRESSING WITH STONE CHIPPINGS

As an alternative to asphalt, completely resurface a path or drive with natural stone chippings embedded in fresh bitumen emulsion. Chippings in various colors are available in sacks which cover varied areas depending on weight. Apply weedkiller and fill potholes as for tarmac (see right).

Bitumen emulsion sets by evaporation in about 12 hours, but until that time it is not completely waterproof. So check the weather forecast to avoid wet conditions. You can lay emulsion on a damp surface but not on one that is icy.

Apply emulsion according to the manufacturer's instructions for the type of base you are surfacing.

SURFACE	BITUMEN EMULSION
Concrete and smooth surfaces	2.6 lbs. per sq. yd.
Other firm, dense surfaces	3.4 lbs. per sq. yd.
Open textured, loose surfaces	7.25 lbs. per sq. yd.

Decant the emulsion into a bucket to make it easier to pour onto the surface, brushing it out, not too thinly, with a stiff broom as for laying tarmac (see right). Having brushed out one bucket of emulsion, spread the stone chippings evenly with a spade. Hold the spade horizontally just above the surface and gently shake the chippings off the edge of the blade (**1**). Don't pile them too thickly, but make sure the emulsion is covered completely. Cover an area of about 5 square yards, then roll the chippings down. When the entire area is covered, roll it once more. If traces of bitumen show between the chippings, mask them with sharp sand and roll again. (See margin notes left for applying dressing to heavy-wear areas.)

You can walk or drive on the dressed surface immediately. One week later, gently sweep away any surplus chippings. Patch any bare areas by re-treating them with emulsion and chippings.

Sprinkle a layer of chippings with a spade

RESURFACING WITH TARMAC

Smarten up an old tarmac path or drive, or any basically sound but unsightly paved area, by resurfacing with cold cure tarmac. It makes a serviceable surface and is ready *to lay from the sack. Roll the tarmac flat with a heavy garden roller—a light roller will do, but you will have to make extra passes.*

Choosing the materials

Choose between red or black tarmac. It is available in sacks that will cover up to about 10 square feet at a thickness of about ½ inch. Each sack contains a separate bag of decorative stone chippings for embedding in the soft tarmac as an alternative finish. Cold cure tarmac can be laid in any weather, but it is much easier to level and roll flat on a warm, dry day. If you have to work in cold weather, store the materials in a warm place the night before laying. While not essential, edging the tarmac with bricks, concrete curbs or wooden boards (◁) will improve the appearance of the finished surface.

Preparing the surface

Pull up all weeds and grass growing between the old paving, then apply a strong weedkiller to the surface two days before you lay the tarmac. Sweep the area clean, and level any potholes by first cutting the sides vertical, then remove dust and debris from the hole. Paint with bitumen emulsion, supplied by the tarmac manufacturer. Wait for it to turn black before filling the hole with ¾-inch-thick layers of tarmac, compacting each layer until the surface is level.

Apply a tack coat of bitumen emulsion to the entire surface to make a firm bond between the new tarmac and the old paving. Mask surrounding walls, curb stones and drain gratings. Stir the emulsion with a stick before pouring it from its container, then spread it thinly with a stiff-bristled broom. Try not to splash, and avoid leaving puddles, especially at the foot of a slope. Let the tack coat set for about 20 minutes and, in the meantime, wash the broom in hot, soapy water. Don't apply the tack coat when it is likely to rain.

Apply a tack coat of bitumen emulsion

Applying the tarmac

Rake the tarmac to make a layer about ¾ inch thick (**1**), using a straightedge to scrape the surface flat. Press down any stubborn lumps with your foot. Spread the contents of no more than three sacks before the initial rolling. Keep the roller set (**2**) to avoid picking up specks of tarmac. Don't run the roller onto grass or gravel or you may roll particles into the tarmac.

Spread and roll tarmac over the whole area, then achieve the final compaction by rolling it thoroughly in several directions. Lightly scatter the chippings (**3**) prior to the final pass.

You can walk on the tarmac immediately, but avoid wearing high-heeled shoes. Don't drive on it for a day or two, and leave a note on the gate to warn others that the paving is not completely cured. You should always protect tarmac from oil and gasoline spillage, but take special care while the surface is fresh.

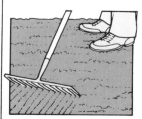
1 Level the tarmac

2 Keep the roller wet

3 Scatter chippings

BUILDING GARDEN STEPS

Designing a garden for a sloping site is an exciting challenge. It offers many possibilities for interesting changes of level by terracing areas of paving or with planting beds held in place with retaining walls (▷). But to move safely from one level to another requires at least one flight of steps.

Designing steps

If you are fortunate enough to own a large garden, and the slope is very gradual, a series of steps with wide treads and low risers can make an impressive feature. If the slope is steep, you can avoid a staircase appearance by constructing a flight of steps composed of a few treads interposed with wide, flat landings, at which points the flight can change direction to add further interest and offer a different viewpoint of the garden. In fact, a shallow flight can be virtually a series of landings, perhaps circular in plan, gradually sweeping up the slope in a curve.

The proportion of tread (the part you stand on) to riser (the vertical part of the step) is an important factor if using the steps is to be both safe and comfortable. As a rough guide, construct steps so that the depth of the tread (from front to back) plus twice the height of the riser equals 26 inches. For example, 12-inch treads should be matched with 7-inch risers, 14-inch treads with 6-inch risers and so on. Never make treads less than 12 inches deep or risers higher than 7 inches.

Garden steps built with natural stone

Using concrete slabs

Concrete paving units in their various forms (▷) are ideal for making firm, flat treads for garden steps. Construct the risers from concrete facing blocks or bricks, allowing the treads to overhang by an inch or two to cast an attractive shadow line which also defines the edge of the step.

Measure the difference in height from the top of the slope to the bottom to gauge the number of steps required. Mark the positions of the risers with pegs and roughly shape the steps in the soil as confirmation (**1**).

Either lay concrete slabs, bedded in sand (▷), flush with the ground at the foot of the slope or dig a trench to contain gravel and a 4- to 6-inch concrete base to support the first riser (**2**). When the concrete has set, construct the riser using normal bricklaying methods (▷). Check its alignment with a level (**3**). Fill behind the riser with compacted gravel until it is level, then lay the tread on a bed of mortar (**4**). Using a level as a guide, tap down the tread until it slopes very slightly towards its front edge to shed rainwater and so prevent ice from forming in cold weather.

Measure from the front edge of the tread to mark the position of the next riser on the slabs (**5**), and construct the step in the same way. Set the final tread flush with the area of paving, pathway or lawn at the top of the flight of steps.

Dealing with the sides

It is usually possible to landscape the slope at each side of the flight of steps, and turf or plant it to prevent the soil from washing down onto the steps. Alternatively, extend the riser to edge each tread or build a wall or planter on each side of the steps. Another solution is to retain the soil from with large stones, perhaps extending into a rock garden on one or both sides.

I Cut the shape of the steps in the soil

2 Dig the footing for the first riser

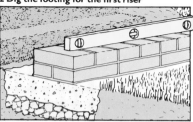

3 Build a brick riser and level it

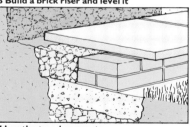

4 Lay the tread on mortar

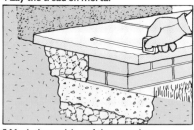

5 Mark the position of the next riser

SEE ALSO

Details for: ▷	
Mixing mortar	27
Footings	29
Laying bricks	**30–31**
Retaining walls	**39**
Paving units	**48**
Laying in sand	**50**

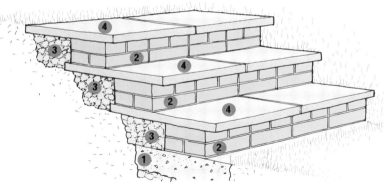

Concrete-slab steps
A section through a simple flight of garden steps built with bricks and concrete paving slabs.
1 Concrete footing
2 Brick-built riser
3 Gravel fill
4 Concrete-slab tread

REPAIRING CONCRETE STEPS

Casting new steps in concrete needs such complicated formwork that the end result hardly justifies the amount of effort required, especially when better-looking steps can be constructed from cast concrete slabs and blocks. Nevertheless, if you have a flight of concrete steps in your garden you will want to keep them in good condition. Like other forms of masonry, concrete suffers from spalling, where frost breaks down the surface and flakes off fragments of material. It occurs a great deal along the front edges of steps where foot traffic adds to the problem. Repair broken edges as soon as you can. Not only are they ugly, but the steps are not as safe as they might be.

Building up broken edges

Wearing safety goggles, chip away concrete around the damaged area and provide a good grip for fresh concrete. Cut a board to match the height of the riser and prop it against the step with bricks (**1**). Mix up a small batch of general-purpose concrete but add a little PVA bonding agent to help it stick to the damaged steps. Dilute some bonding agent with water, say 3 parts water: 1 part bonding agent, and brush it onto the damaged area, stippling it into all the crevices. When the painted surface becomes tacky, fill the hole with concrete mix flush with the edge of the board (**2**). Round the front edge slightly with a homemade edging float (◁), running it against the board (**3**).

● **Dealing with slippery steps**
Algae will grow in damp conditions, especially under trees, and steps can become dangerously slippery if it is allowed to build up on the surfaces. Brush with a solution of 1 part household bleach: 4 parts water. After 48 hours, wash with clean water and repeat if the fungal growth is heavy. You can also use a proprietary fungicidal solution, but follow manufacturers' instructions carefully.

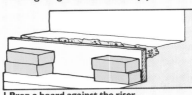

1 Prop a board against the riser

2 Fill the front edge with concrete

3 Run an edging float against the board

CURVED STEPS/LOG STEPS

Building curved steps

To build a series of curved steps, choose materials which will make the job as easy as possible. You can use tapered concrete slabs (◁) for the treads, designing the circumference of the steps to suit the proportions of the slabs. Or, you can contruct the treads from crazy paving (◁), selecting fairly large stones for the front edge. Use bricks laid flat or on edge to build the risers. Set the bricks to radiate from the center of the curve, and fill the slightly tapered joints with mortar.

Use a length of string attached to a peg driven into the ground as an improvised compass to mark out the curve of each step. Tie a stake to the string to help you gauge the front edge of the lower steps (**1**). Roughly shape the soil and lay a concrete foundation for the bottom riser (◁). Build risers and treads as for regular concrete slab steps, using the improvised string compass as a guide.

Building circular landings

To construct a circular landing, build the front edge with bricks and paving as for a curved step. When the mortar has set, fill the landing area with compacted coarse gravel (◁) and lay pea gravel up to the level of the tread (**2**).

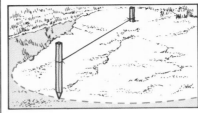

1 Mark the edge with an improvised compass

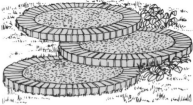

2 Circular landings made with bricks and gravel

Making log steps

For an informal garden, build steps from lengths of logs soaked in a chemical preservative. Try to construct risers of a fairly regular height, otherwise someone might stumble if they are forced to break step. As it is not always possible to obtain uniform logs, you may have to make up the height of the riser with two or more slimmer logs.

Cut a regular slope in the earth bank and compact the soil by treading it down. Drive stakes cut from 3-inch-diameter logs into the ground, one at each end of a step (**1**). Place one heavy log behind the stakes, bedding it down in the soil (**2**), and pack coarse gravel behind it to construct the tread of the step (**3**). Shovel a layer of pea gravel on top of the coarse to finish the step.

If large logs are in short supply, build a step from two or three slim logs, holding them against the stakes with gravel as you construct the riser (**4**).

1 Drive a stake at each end of a step

2 Place a log behind the stakes

3 Fill behind the log with gravel

Log-built garden steps

4 Make up a riser with two slim logs

CREATING WATER GARDENS

There is nothing like still or running water to enliven a garden. Cascades and fountains have an almost mesmeric fascination—it is practically impossible to take your eyes off them—and the sound of trickling water has a charming, soothing effect. Even a small area of still water will support all manner of interesting pond life and plants, with the additional bonus of the mirrored images of trees, rocks and sky reflected in its placid surface.

Pond liners

It is not by chance that the number of garden ponds has increased over recent years. There is no doubt that their popularity is due largely to the emergence of simply installed rigid and flexible pond liners, making it possible to create a complete water garden in return for a few days' work.

In the past it was necessary to line a pond with concrete. While it is true that concrete is a very versatile material, there is always the possibility of a leak developing through cracks caused by ground movement or the force of expanding ice. There are no such worries with flexible liners. In addition to the labor and expense involved in building forms for a concrete pond, it must be left to season for about a month, during which time it must be emptied and refilled a number of times to ensure that the water will be safe for fish and plant life. But you can introduce plants to a plastic- or rubber-lined pool as soon as the water itself has matured, which takes no more than a few days.

Ordering a flexible liner

Use a simple formula to calculate the size of liner you will need. Disregard the actual plan and ignore the size and shape of planting shelves. Simply take the overall length and width of the pond and add twice the maximum depth to each dimension to arrive at the size of the liner. If possible, adapt your design to fall within the nearest stock liner size.

SEE ALSO
Details for: ▷	
Installing liners	58–59
Building a waterfall	61

Garden pond
A well-planted water garden surrounded by flowering shrubs looks like a natural pond.

CHOOSING A POND LINER

The advantages of proprietary pond liners over concrete are fairly clear, but there are still a number of options to choose from, depending on the size and shape of the pond you wish to create and how much you propose to spend.

RIGID LINERS

Regular garden-center visitors will be familiar with the range of preformed plastic pond liners. The best liners are made from rigid glass-reinforced plastic which is very strong and resistant to the effects of frost or ice. As long as they are handled with reasonable care and installed correctly, rigid plastic pools are practically puncture- and leak-proof.

SEMIRIGID LINERS

Semirigid liners, made from vacuum-formed plastic, are cheaper than those made from fiberglass, but the range of sizes is very limited. However, they make ideal reservoirs or header pools for a cascade or waterfall.

Rectangular or irregular-shaped liners are available in rigid or semirigid plastic, and a very acceptable water garden can be created with a carefully selected series of pond liners linked by watercourses.

FLEXIBLE LINERS

For complete freedom of design, choose a flexible-sheet liner designed to stretch and hug the contours of a pond of virtually any shape and size. In addition, a pond made with even the most expensive sheet liner is cheaper to construct and guaranteed to last longer than an equivalent rigid plastic liner.

Polyethylene liners, once the only type of flexible liner on the market, are still available but they are relatively fragile, and should be considered only for temporary pools. And even then, they should be lined with a double thickness of material. PVC liners, especially those reinforced with nylon, are guaranteed for up to 10 years of normal use, but if you want your pond to last for 50 years or more, choose a synthetic rubber membrane based on butyl. Not all butyl liners are of the same quality, so buy one from a reputable manufacturer offering a 20-year written guarantee if you want the very best product. Black and stone-colored butyl liners are made in a wide range of stock sizes, but if you can't find one to suit your needs, you can have one made to order.

Rigid pond liner
Rigid liners are molded using glass-reinforced plastic.

Flexible liners
Best-quality flexible liners are made from butyl.

DESIGNING A POND

A pond must be sited correctly if it is to have any chance of maturing into an attractive, clear stretch of water. Never place a pond under deciduous trees. Falling leaves will pollute the water as they decay, causing fish to become ill and even die. Some trees are especially poisonous.

Positioning for sunlight

A pond must receive plenty of daylight. Although sunlight promotes the growth of algae, which causes ponds to turn a pea-green color, it is also necessary to encourage the growth of other water plant life. An abundant growth of oxygenating plants will compete with the algae for the mineral salts and, with shade provided by floating and marginal plants, will keep the pond clear.

Size and shape

The proportion of the pond is important in creating harmony between plants and fish. It is difficult to maintain the right conditions for clear water in a pond less than 40 square feet in surface area, but the volume of water is even more vital. A pond up to about 100 square feet in area should be 18 inches deep. As the area increases, you will have to dig deeper to about 24 inches or more, but it is rarely necessary to go below 30 inches.

A flexible liner will conform better to simple curves, but the section or profile must be designed to fulfill certain requirements. To grow marginal plants, you will need a 9-inch-wide shelf around the edge of the pond, 9 inches below the surface of the water. This will take a standard 6-inch planting flat with ample water above, and you can always raise the flat on pieces of paving or bricks. The sides of the pond should slope at about 20 degrees to prevent soil collapse during construction and to allow the liner to stretch without promoting too many creases. It will also allow a sheet of ice to float upwards without damaging the liner. Judge the angle by measuring 3 inches inwards for every 9 inches of depth. If the soil is very sandy, increase the angle of slope slightly for extra stability.

Accommodating a sloping site

On a sloping site, build up the low side with earth, turfing up to the paving surround. Cut back the higher side and build a low retaining wall, or bed stones against the earth to create a rock garden.

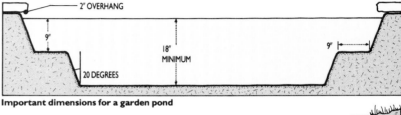

Important dimensions for a garden pond

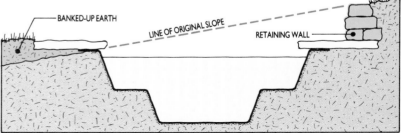

Accommodating a sloping site

Installing a rigid liner

Stand up a rigid liner in position and prop it up with cardboard boxes, both to check its orientation and to mark its perimeter on the ground. Use a level to plot key points on the ground (**1**) and mark them with small stakes. You will need to dig outside this line, so absolute accuracy is not required.

As you move the topsoil, either take it away in a wheelbarrow or pile it close by ready to incorporate into a rock garden. Lay a straightedge across the top and measure the depth of the excavation (**2**), including marginal shelves. Keep the excavation as close as possible to the shape of the liner, but extend it by 6 inches on all sides. Compact the base and cover it with a 1-inch-deep level of sharp sand. Lower the liner down and bed it firmly into the sand. Check that the pool stands level (**3**) and wedge it temporarily with wooden stakes until the back-fill of soil or sand can hold it.

Start to fill the liner with water from a hose and, at the same time, pour sifted soil or sand behind the liner (**4**). There is no need to hurry as it will take some time to fill, but keep pace with the level of the water. Reach into the excavation and pack soil under the marginal shelves with your hands.

When the liner is firmly bedded in the soil, either finish the edge with stones as for a flexible liner (see opposite) or re-lay turf to cover the rim of the liner.

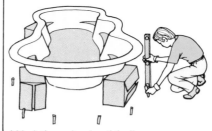

1 Mark the perimeter of the liner

2 Measure the depth of the excavation

3 Make sure the liner stands level

4 Backfill with sifted soil or sand

CONSTRUCTING A POND: FLEXIBLE LINER

Excavating the pond

Mark out the shape of the pond on the ground. A garden hose is useful for trying out curvilinear shapes. Excavate the pond to the level of the planting shelf, then mark and dig out the deeper sections (1). Remove sharp stones and roots from the sides and base to make sure they won't puncture the liner.

The top of the pond must be level, and the surrounding stone or concrete slabs must be ¾ inch below the turf. For those reasons, cut back the turf to accommodate the stones and then drive wooden reference stakes into the exposed surround every 3 to 4 feet. Level the tops of all the stakes using a straightedge (2) and check the level across the pond as well. Remove or pack earth around the stakes until the compacted soil is level below them.

When the surround is level, remove the stakes and spread ½ inch of slightly damp sand over the base and sides of the excavation (3).

Installing a flexible liner

Drape the liner across the excavation with an even overlap all round, and hold it in place with bricks while you fill the pond with water from a hose (4). It will take several hours to fill a large pond, but check it regularly, moving the bricks as the liner stretches. A few creases are inevitable around sharp curves but you will lose most of them by keeping the liner fairly taut and easing it into shape as the water rises. Turn off the water when the level reaches about 2 inches below the edge of the pond. Cut off surplus liner with scissors, leaving a 6-inch overlap all round (5). Push 4-inch nails through the overlap into the soil so that the liner cannot slip while you place the edging stones.

Building the surround

Lay flat stones dry at first, selecting those which follow the shape of the pond with a reasonably close fit between them. Let the stones project over the water by about 2 inches to cast a deep shadow line and reflection. Cut stones with a bolster to fit the gaps behind the larger edging stones (▷). Lift the stones one or two at a time and bed them on two or three strategically placed mounds of mortar mixed with 1 part cement: 3 parts soft sand (6). Tap the stones level with a mallet and fill the joints with a trowel. Smooth the joints flush with an old paintbrush. Do not drop mortar in the water or you will have to empty and refill the pond before you introduce fish or plants.

INCORPORATING A DRAIN

The recommended water level for a pond is about 2 inches below the edging stones, but in exceptional circumstances such as a heavy storm, or if you forget to turn off the water when topping up, the water can rise fast enough to spill over and flood the garden. As a precaution, build a drain beneath the edging stones to allow excess water to escape. Not only does a drain prevent a flood, it provides a means of running electric cable into the pond to power a pump or lighting. Cut corrugated plastic sheet into two strips 6 inches wide and long enough to run under the edging stones. Pop-rivet the strips together to make a channel about an inch deep (1). Scrape earth and sand from beneath the liner to accommodate the channel (2), then lay edging stones on top to hold it in place. Dig a small soakaway behind the channel and fill it with rubble topped with fine gravel or turf up to the level of the stones.

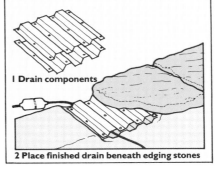

1 Drain components

2 Place finished drain beneath edging stones

1 Dig the excavation as accurately as possible

2 Level the edge using reference stakes

3 Line the excavation with damp sand

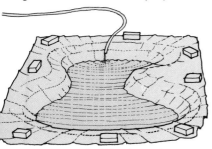

4 Stretch the liner by filling the pond

5 Cut the flexible liner to fit

6 Lay edging stones to complete the pond

MAKING A RAISED-EDGE POND

You can build a formal pond with a raised edge using bricks or concrete facing blocks. An edging about 18 inches high is safer for small children while also providing seating for adults. If you prefer a low wall—say, 9 inches high—create planting shelves at ground level, digging the pond deeper in the center. Place planting crates on blocks around the edge of a deep raised pond.

Building the pond

Lay 4- to 6-inch concrete footings (◁) to support the walls, which are constructed from two skins of masonry set apart to match the width of flat coping stones. Allow for an overhang of 2 inches over the water's edge and lap the outer wall by ½ to ¾ inch. To save money, build the inner wall from plain concrete blocks or cheap common bricks, reserving more expensive and decorative bricks or facing blocks for the outer skin of the wall. Raised ponds can be lined with a standard flexible liner or you can order a prefabricated fitted liner to reduce the amount of creasing at the corners. Trap the edge of whichever liner you select under the coping stones.

Raised-edge pond
A well-designed and constructed pond which is nicely integrated in a sloping site.

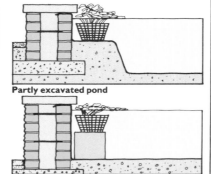

Partly excavated pond

Fully raised pond built with a cavity wall

Pumps and fountains

Small submersible pumps for fountains and waterfalls are operated either directly from the house electrical supply or through a transformer which reduces the voltage to 12 volts. The combination of house electricity and water can be fatal, so consult an electrician if you plan to use a 12-volt pump. A low-voltage pump is safe and can be installed and wired simply (◁).

Place the pump in the water and run its electric cable beneath the edging stones, preferably via a drain (◁), to a waterproof connector attached to the extension lead of a transformer installed inside the house. This permits removal of the pump for servicing without disturbing the extension cable or transformer. Run pumps regularly, even in the winter months, to keep them in good working order, and clean both the pump and its filter according to the manufacturer's instructions.

There are so many waterfall pumps and fountain kits available that you should consult manufacturers' catalogues to find one that best suits your purpose. Place a submersible waterfall pump close to the edge of the pond so that you can reach it to disconnect the hose running to the waterfall when you need to service the pump. Stand fountain units on a flat stone or propped up on bricks so that the jet is vertical. Plant water lilies some distance away from a fountain as falling water will encourage the flowers to close up.

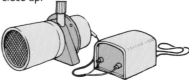

Low-voltage waterfall pump and transformer

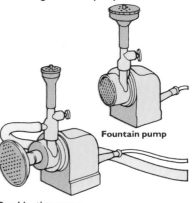

Fountain pump

Combination pump

ALTERNATIVE POND EDGING

Edging a pond with flat stones provides a safe and attractive footpath for tending to water plants and fish, but a more natural setting is often required, particularly for small header pools in a rock garden. Incorporate a shelf around the pond as for marginal plants, but this time for an edging of rocks. If you place them carefully there is no need to mortar them. Arrange rocks behind the edging to cover the liner (**1**).

To create a shallow, beachlike edging, slope the soil at a very shallow angle and lay large pebbles or flat rocks upon the liner. You can merge them with a rock garden or let them form a natural water line (**2**).

To discourage neighborhood cats from poaching fish from a pond, create an edging of trailing plants. Without a firm foothold, no cat will attempt to reach into the water. Bed a strip of soft wire netting in the mortar below flat edging stones. Cut the strip to overhang the water by about 6 inches as a support for the plants (**3**). Once the plants are established, they will disguise the nature of the pool liner.

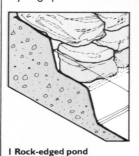

1 Rock-edged pond

2 Pebble-strewn shelf

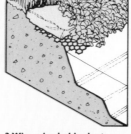

3 Wire edge holds plants

BUILDING A ROCK GARDEN AND WATERFALL

A waterfall, complemented by a rock garden displaying clumps of ferns or graceful shrubs and trees such as Japanese maple or dwarf conifers, adds a further dimension to a water garden. The technique for building a series of watercourses is not as complicated as it may appear and, in doing so, you can also cover much of the groundwork needed for your rock garden.

Materials

You will be surprised by the amount of soil produced by excavating a pond. To avoid the waste and trouble of transporting it to a local dump, use it to create your poolside rock garden. If you include a small reservoir on the higher ground you can pump water into it from the main pond to be returned via a trickling cascade or waterfall.

You'll have plenty of soil, but obtaining enough stones to give the impression of a real rocky outcrop can be very expensive, that is, if you buy them from a local garden center. A cheaper way is to use hollow, cast reproduction rocks, which surprisingly will eventually weather-in quite well. However, your best option is to buy natural stone direct from a quarry.

Real rocks can be extremely heavy, so have them delivered as close to the site as possible, and have a sturdy cart on hand to move individual stones about the garden. A rock garden and waterfall are actually built as one operation but for the sake of clarity, they are described separately here.

AVOIDING STRAIN

Lifting stones
Keep your back straight when lifting heavy stones (right). Use a rope to lift and place large rocks (below).

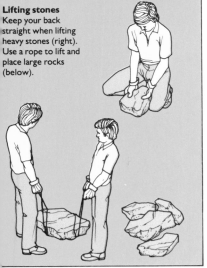

Creating a waterfall

So that the waterfall can discharge directly into the main pond, form a small inlet at the side of the pond by leaving a large flap of flexible liner. Build shallow banks at each side of the inlet and line them with stones (1). Create a stepped watercourse ascending in stages to the reservoir. Line the watercourse with cutoffs of flexible liner which must be overlapped on the face of each waterfall. Tuck the edge of each lower piece of liner under the edge of the piece above, and hold them in place with stones. To retain water in small pools along the watercourse, cut each step with a slope toward the rear (2), placing stones along the lip for the desired effect (3). A flat stone gives a sheet of water whereas a layer of pebbles produces a rippling cascade.

Test the watercourse as the construction work progresses by running water from a hose—it is difficult to adjust the angle of stones once the watercourse has been completed.

Bury the flexible hose from the waterfall pump in the rockery, making sure there are no sharp bends which would restrict the flow of water. Cut the hose so that it emerges at the edge of the reservoir and cover it with a flat stone (4) to hold and hide it.

A rigid plastic reservoir will have a lip molded in an edge which will allow water to escape down the watercourse. If you construct a reservoir with flexible liner, however, shape the edge to form a low point and support a flat stone over the opening to hide the liner (5).

SEE ALSO

Details for: ▷

Obtaining stone	22
Flexible liners	57

Cascade or waterfall
This section shows a cascade or waterfall running from a reservoir to a pond.
1 Pond inlet
2 Watercourse step
3 Overhanging stone creates a sheet of water
4 Hose from pump
5 Reservoir outlet
6 Reservoir

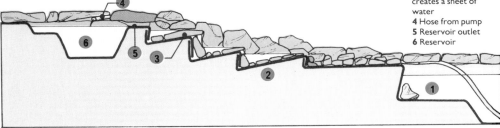

Constructing a rock garden

Select and place each stone in a rockery to create an illusion of strata, or layers, of rock. Stones placed haphazardly at odd angles tend to resemble a spoil heap rather than a natural outcrop. Take care not to strain yourself when lifting rocks. Keep your feet together and use your leg muscles to do the work, keeping your back as straight as possible. To move a particularly heavy rock, slip a rope around it (see left).

Lay large flat rocks to form the front edge of the rockery, placing soil behind

and between them to form a flat, level platform. Compact the soil to make sure there are no air pockets which will damage the roots of plants. Lay subsequent layers of rock set back from the first, but not in a regular pattern. Place some to create steep embankments, others to form a gradual slope of wide steps. Pockets of soil for planting alpines or other small plants will form naturally as you lay the stones, but plan larger areas of soil for specimen shrubs or dwarf trees.

Building a rock garden
A rockery should have irregular rock steps along its front edge.

Incorporating a bog garden

An area of wet, boggy soil where specialized waterside plants will flourish complements a pond perfectly. When you excavate the pond, make a wide planting shelf covered with the flexible liner. Place a row of stones to form the edge of the pond, dividing the bog area from the deep water. Bed the stones in 2 inches of mortar. When the mortar has set, its lime content must be neutralized by painting on a solution of

waterproof powder available from pond specialists. Follow manufacturers' instructions for its use.

Incorporate the bog garden into a rockery by lining the perimeter with stones, then fill the area with soil. The liner beneath the soil will retain enough moisture to keep the garden permanently damp, but make sure the planting bed is deep enough to ensure plants are not waterlogged.

Bog garden
Construct a bog garden next to a pond for waterside plants.

INSTALLING OUTDOOR WIRING

If you can do your own wiring inside your home, you can certainly do it outside as well. The principles are the same. Because outdoor wiring is exposed to all kinds of weather, it must be impervious to water. It must also be resistant to the effects of extreme hot and cold temperatures. Knowing how to work with these materials is most of what you need to know to run electricity outdoors.

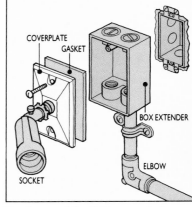

Tapping an existing light or receptacle

Connecting to the house circuits

You can bring indoor electricity outside with one of two exterior fittings:

90° fittings
If you are starting with a new circuit in the breaker panel or tapping into an existing circuit with a junction box, the fitting you will use to get through the house wall will be an LB, or conduit (◁). (An LB cannot be installed underground, however.) An LB allows you to come through an exterior wall and make a 90-degree turn along the wall. It is threaded on each end to accept conduit adapters or pipe nipples. Because it creates a 90-degree turn, its front can be removed so that you can help the wires make the turn. The coverplate for this opening fits over a rubber gasket, which makes the box water tight.

An LB is always installed between two pieces of conduit. In some cases, an LB might fit back-to-back with an outlet box, with the outlet box just inside the wall and the LB flush with the outside. Because no splices with plastic connectors are allowed inside smaller LB's, the conversion between cabled wire and individual wire should be made inside the junction box.

If you choose to run buriable cable inside the conduit instead of individual wires, a plastic connector conversion will not be necessary. In that case, a junction box inside the wall will not be necessary either. The LB could just be fastened to a short nipple through the wall. You could then run buriable cable uninterrupted from the panel to its first box. If you wish to exit a basement wall below ground level, do not use an LB. Use instead, a junction box mounted to the inside wall, then run conduit through the wall.

Extension boxes
If you are tapping into an outside outlet or light, you will not need an LB. Instead you can sandwich a weatherproof extension box between a receptacle, or fixture, and its outlet box.

To install an extension box, shut the power off, remove the coverplate and receptacle or fixture and pull the wires out of the box. Then screw the extension box to the outlet box mounted in the wall. Bring the conduit into the extension box and pull the conduit wires through the opening so that you can work on them comfortably. Connect all corresponding wires with plastic connectors and pigtail over to the receptacle or fixture. In this way, the existing circuit still serves the receptacle or fixture, but also serves the new wiring in the conduit. Then ground the outlet (◁) and replace the existing receptacle or fixture using the weathertight gaskets provided (◁).

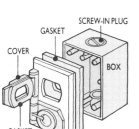

Features of an outdoor receptacle box

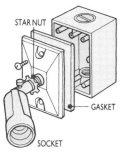

Features of an outdoor floodlight box

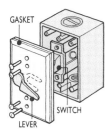

Uses a standard switch with an external lever

Connecting a new circuit
A box extender and metal conduit.

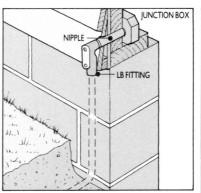

An LB allows you to wire at a 90° angle

An LB and a junction box back-to-back

WORKING BEYOND THE HOUSE

All outdoor wiring must be encased in conduit unless it is buried 30 inches deep. All fixtures and boxes, including switch and receptacle boxes, must be weathertight and rated for exterior use. And all floodlights and their sockets must be rated for exterior use. As long as you satisfy these requirements, the improvements you make can be as varied as your outdoor needs.

LOW-VOLTAGE ALTERNATIVES

Low-voltage wiring was once limited to doorbells and thermostats (▷). Today, however, low-voltage lighting is being used in places unheard of a generation ago. The reason, of course, is that low-voltage systems give you more light for less money, and rising electric rates have made efficiency an issue. Low-voltage wiring is also safe, if you short circuit a low-voltage system, the shock you get will feel more like a tickle than the life-threatening bite of a 120-volt system.

There are literally dozens of low-voltage lighting systems available today. You can run tiny low-voltage lights under the tread of each step in a stairway. You can run a string of mini-lights along a beam. You can highlight a favorite wall hanging or work of art with low-voltage track lighting. You can even frame the object with lights that have barn doors and focusing lenses. And finally, you can install low-voltage landscape lighting in your back yard that costs you only pennies a day to operate. If you've got something special in mind, you can do it with low-voltage systems already on the market.

Low-voltage kits

The best way to buy low-voltage components is in kit form. You won't necessarily save money that way, but you won't have to design your own system either. When you buy a kit, for example, the transformer size, the length and size of the wire and the number of allowable fixtures is all figured for you. If you install the kit according to instructions, you won't run the risk of over extending the system.

Contrary to popular opinion, low-voltage systems can start fires when over-extended. Too many fixtures or too long a run can cause low-voltage wires to overheat. If you hope to design your own system, make sure you use a transformer with a built-in breaker.

If you don't find exactly the combination of features you want in one brand, try another brand or another style. Track lighting offers a good illustration of this point. You can get a fixture that fastens to the ceiling and has a surface cord that runs to a transformer that you plug into a socket. You can find one the same size with a surface-mounted transformer that ties to a ceiling box. And you can find one that has a transformer hidden in a recessed fixture so that you can't see it at all. Kit lights need not limit your design options.

Installing a transformer

In order to reduce your house current from 120 volts to 12 volts, a transformer will be needed. There are several sizes of transformers to meet a variety of needs. Most transformers used in residential wiring are rated at 100 to 300 watts. The greater the rating, the more 100-foot branch circuits can be served. If a transformer is underrated, the lights it serves will not go on or the wire that serves them will overheat.

As mentioned earlier, transformers for indoor fixtures can be located in a number of places on or near their fixtures. In some fixtures, they can be part of an electronic circuit, similar to that of a stereo. But in many cases, you will fasten the transformer directly to a 120-volt metal outlet box. Just remove a knockout plug and fasten the transformer to the box with a clamp.

Then fasten the leads from the transformer to pigtail connections inside the box. The low-voltage UF wires can then be tied to the terminals of the transformer.

A transformer designed to be used outdoors, however, must be sealed in its own weathertight box. You can buy transformers with on/off switches built in, or you can use a conventional switch between the outlet and the transformer. The transformer box must be connected to the outlet box with weathertight conduit (▷). Then, from the transformer, low-voltage UF cable should be laid underground to each fixture. Low-voltage fixtures do not need to be grounded and because they pose no physical threat, do not have to be buried deep or encased in conduit when installed outdoors. Keep them out of harm's way, however.

Low-voltage fixture connections

Low-voltage connections are made inside protective boxes on indoor lighting fixtures. In some cases, the low-voltage side of the fixture is wired and sealed at the factory. When you install these fixtures, you will only have to wire the 120-volt connection. Terminals on the low-voltage side of a transformer can remain exposed provided the transformer is not covered by drywall or otherwise concealed.

All outdoor connectors must be made inside weathertight boxes (▷), of course. They can be made the conventional way with binding screws or with special low-voltage connectors. These connectors use a screw-and-clamp device. The cable is placed in a slot and the clamp is screwed down over it. As the clamp tightens, it pierces the cable, making contact with the wires inside. In this case, you do not even have to cut the wire at the fixture. Both connections are legal in outdoor installations provided they take place in weathertight boxes.

SEE ALSO
Details for: ▷
Installation   62

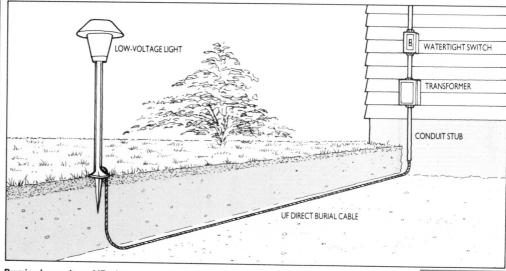

Burying low-voltage UF wire
Low-voltage UF wire can be buried without conduit after it reaches ground level.

LOW-VOLTAGE LIGHT

WATERTIGHT SWITCH

TRANSFORMER

CONDUIT STUB

UF DIRECT BURIAL CABLE

INFESTATION: INSECTS

Our homes and surroundings are often invaded by various voracious insect pests. Some of them are quite harmless, although they cause a great deal of annoyance and even alarm, but certain insects can seriously weaken the structure *of a building and it is these pests which often go unnoticed until the damage is done. At the first signs of infestation, try to identify and eradicate the cause as quickly as possible, before it escalates, causing even further damage.*

Termites

Termites are wood-eating insects, prevalent in nearly all parts of the country. Although if neglected they can cause severe damage, infestation is easily eradicable by professional pest-control experts and can be prevented in many cases by incorporating special, relatively inexpensive building techniques during construction.

Of the three significant species of termites in the U.S.—*subterranean*, *damp-wood*, and *dry-wood*—the subterranean variety do the most damage. These ¼-inch-long pests live underground—often at depths of up to 25 feet—and travel to the surface for food. They eat only cellulose, the material of wood fiber, and must avoid both light and the drying effects of open air. If they are shut off from moisture—which they receive by living in the ground—they die in only a few days.

Termites colonize as ants do, and their societies are formed of groups of specialized members. Within a colony there are winged termites, whose job it

is to reproduce, and wingless termites, some of which act as soldiers and defend the colony, and others of which are workers, whose job it is to construct tunnels and forage for food. It is the workers which do the most damage.

Because termites avoid light, they feed entirely within the wood they find, so their presence is often hard to detect. As they travel upward from their nests, they feed on any wood in contact with the ground, and will sometimes build earth-covered tunnels several inches up the sides of impervious material such as masonry foundation walls or pipes to reach still higher. They can also burrow through weak mortar joints and poorly laid concrete.

Once a year, in spring or early summer, the winged, reproductive termites swarm, leaving their nest to fly to a new location to found another colony. Often the migration takes place only for a few hours. At the new site, the termites drop their wings and tunnel underground.

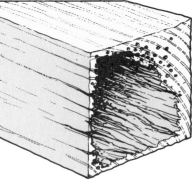
Termites feed only on interior wood

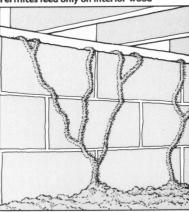
Termite tunnels along foundation wall

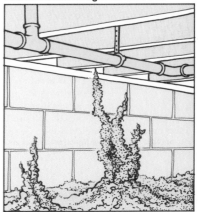
Freestanding termite tunnels

Damp-wood termite

Damp-wood and dry-wood termites

Damp-wood termites do not require soil moisture. They may reach 1 inch in length and have a 2-inch wingspan. They inhabit only moisture-soaked wood and presently are a problem only along the Pacific coast.

Dry-wood termites resemble subterraneans, but require very little moisture to survive. Instead of dwelling underground, they bore directly into

above-ground wood—even furniture—then plug their holes behind them as they begin to colonize. Currently, dry-wood termites are not a widespread problem in the U.S.—they threaten only a narrow zone along the Atlantic and Gulf coasts south from Virginia, the lower portions of Texas and the southwest, and the Pacific coast as far as northern California.

Termites
1 Winged adult
2 Soldier
3 Worker
4 Queen
5 King

Identifying termites

Winged subterranean termites are sometimes mistaken for flying ants, and vice versa, but the two can be distinguished by inspecting their wings and bodies. Termites have 4 equal-size wings. Flying ants also have 4 wings, but one pair is smaller than the other. Characteristic of ants' bodies is their distinctive pinched-in waist, separating their bodies into distinct sections—thorax and abdomen. Termites have thick waists and,

compared to ants, their body sections are harder to distinguish.

Winged termites, like ants, are dark-colored (sometimes even black) and have completely formed, hard-walled bodies. Soldier termites are also dark. They have large, hard heads, strong jaws and strong legs, but their bodies are soft. They are blind. Workers are blind, too. Their bodies are pale yellow, grayish or white, and almost completely soft.

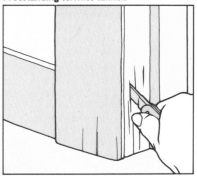
Probe suspect wood with penknife

INSECT INFESTATION

Locating termites

Termite inspections are required as part of most house sales, particularly when a mortgage is involved. In areas where infestation is common, once- or twice-yearly inspections should be made as well, although termites progress slowly and severe damage may take 2 or more years to develop. Here is where and how to look for termites:

Search for tunnels leading from moist earth towards a wood supply. Termite tunnels are half-round, approximately ¼ to ½ inch in diameter, and appear as if made of cement. Normally tunnels are attached to some other surface, but in some instances they may be freestanding. Inspect foundation walls (inside and out), pipes rising from damp earth, and piers. Also check for evidence around foundation cracks, pipe openings, and especially sill joints—where the wood walls of a house rest on top of the foundation. Inspect the seams where concrete patio, garage, or basement slabs meet the house. Also check around basement windowsills and crawlspace ventilators.

Examine any wood that is in contact with the ground for direct entry of termites. Such sites include the bottoms of wooden stairs and railings, fence posts, trellises, firewood and lumber piles, even dead tree stumps.

In spring and early summer, watch for swarms of flying insects which may be termites. They normally enter wood at points near ground level, such as around house foundations, and leave piles of discarded wings at the entrance to the new colony.

Testing for damage

Because termite damage is seldom visible, probe suspect wood with a penknife, screwdriver, or ice pick. If the tool penetrates the wood easily to a depth of ½ inch or more, damage is present. Pry away a portion of the soft wood. If this procedure uncovers chambers or cavities, suspect termites or other wood-boring insects. If the wood seems intact but is uniformly spongy, most likely the problem is not termites, but rot.

Sources of termite infestation
1 Foundation too low
2 Sill and joists contact soil
3 Soil heaped against pier
4 Wood framing contacts soil
5 Porch and steps contact soil
6 Firewood, construction scraps left on dirt basement floor
7 Post extends through concrete
8 Exterior wood siding too near grade
9 Wood framing around vent contacts soil
10 Softened, cracked lime mortar in old brick wall
11 Improper roof drainage (runoff collects around foundation)
12 Loose stucco
13 Cracks in concrete slab floor
14 Unshielded girder end
15 Wood framing beneath chimney (heat attracts termites)
16 Insufficient crawlspace height
17 Rotting stumps and lumber scraps in yard
18 Untreated fence posts and clothesline posts contact soil

Control measures

Once termites are present, the only effective method of extermination is by treating the soil with chemicals to create a toxic envelope surrounding the house. Chlordane is the chemical used most often. Although the purchase of chlordane and other termite-controlling chemicals is still legal, their use may be banned in some regions of the country, or restricted to application only by licensed professionals. Pest-control poisons are hazardous and difficult both to handle safely and apply effectively. If you suspect or locate termite damage, contact a reputable extermination company for assistance.

TERMITE SHIELDS

Incorporating metal termite shields between foundation walls and wood sills, and around pipes entering the soil from the house structure above, is an effective way to prevent termite infestation. In addition, foundation walls should extend at least 6 inches above ground level, and the distance between joists and soil in crawlspaces should be a minimum of 18 inches.

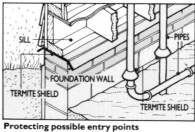

Protecting possible entry points

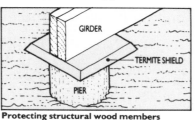

Protecting structural wood members

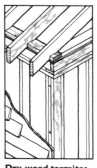

Dry-wood termites often invade attics
They can be controlled by fumigation with nontoxic silica gel dust which dehydrates (and thus kills) them.

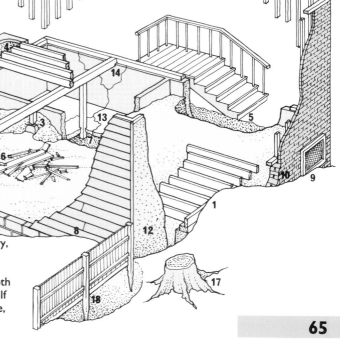

ERADICATING INSECT PESTS

Insecticides can be dangerous if allowed to contaminate food and they are also harmful to honey bees, so follow the manufacturer's instructions carefully when using them to eradicate insect pests of any kind.

Typical household pests
(Not to scale)
The insects shown below are more of a nuisance and a health hazard than a threat to the structure of your house.

Common black ant

Wasp

Housefly

Cockroach

Silverfish

ANTS

The common black ant will enter a house foraging for food. Once established, the workers follow well-defined trails. In summer, great numbers of winged ants emerge from the nest to mate but the swarming is over in a matter of hours, and the ants themselves are harmless. If winged ants stray into the house, they can be overcome with an aerosol insecticidal spray.

To locate the nest, follow the trail of ants. It will be situated under a path, at the base of a wall, in the lawn or under a flat stone, perhaps 20 feet from the house. Destroy the nest by pouring boiling water into the entrances. If this will damage plants, use an insecticidal dust or spray.

WASPS

Wasps are beneficial in spring and early summer, as they feed on garden pests, but later in the year they destroy soft fruit. They will also kill bees and raid the hive for honey. Wasps sting when aroused or frightened.

Trap foraging wasps in open jam jars containing a mixture of jam, water and detergent. Flying wasps can be killed with an aerosol fly spray.

You can destroy wasps at the nest by depositing insecticidal powder near the entrances and areas where insects alight. Approaching a nest can be hazardous, so tie a spoon to a long stick to extend your reach. Alternatively, use a smoke generator where there is no risk of fire. Light a pellet, place it in the entrance and seal the opening.

Treat a wasp sting with a cold compress soaked in witch hazel or use an antihistamine cream or spray.

FLIES

Depending on the species, flies breed in rotting vegetables, manure, decaying meat and offal. They can carry the eggs of parasitic worms and spread disease by leaving small black spots of vomit and excreta on foodstuffs.

Cover food and keep refuse sealed in newspaper or plastic bin liners. Tight-fitting window screens and bead curtain hung in open doorways will prevent flies from entering the house.

An aerosol fly spray will deal with small numbers, but for swarming flies in a roof space, for instance, use an insecticidal smoke generator from a hardware store or agricultural supply store. Large numbers in a living room can be sucked into a vacuum cleaner: Suck up some insecticidal powder and wait a few hours before emptying the bag.

COCKROACHES

Cockroaches can appear anywhere there's a supply of food and water in warm conditions. Cockroaches are unhygienic, and smell unpleasant.

Being nocturnal feeders, cockroaches hide during the day in crevices in walls, behind cupboards and especially under cookers, fridges or near central heating pipes, where it is warmest. A serious outbreak should be dealt with by a professional, but you can lay a finely dusted barrier of insecticidal powder between suspected daytime haunts and supplies of food. Don't sprinkle insecticides near food itself. Use a paintbrush to stipple powder into crevices and under baseboards. When you have eradicated the pests, fill all cracks and gaps to prevent their return.

SILVERFISH

Silverfish are tapered, wingless insects about ½ inch long. They like moist conditions found in kitchens, bathrooms and cellars. You may find them behind wallpaper, where they feed on the paste, or in bookshelves because they also eat paper. Use an insecticidal spray or powder in these locations.

CARPENTER ANTS

Damage from carpenter ants is often mistaken for termite infestation. However, ants tunnel only to construct nesting places; they remove excavated wood to the outside of their nests and keep the passageways clear. Termite galleries, on the other hand, are packed with sawdustlike material which is actually woody feces. This difference in the appearance of infested areas is a positive means of identifying which pest is at work.

Carpenter ants may be seen entering and leaving wood. They vary widely in size but a common variety is approximately ½ inch long, and either all black or mixed with brown. All members of a colony are fully formed except the larvae, which are white and resemble grubs. Small, isolated colonies can be eradicated by injecting pesticide dust into the galleries or into holes drilled at intervals along infested timber. For best results, hire a licensed, professional exterminator.

Winged adult   **Worker**

CARPENTER BEES

Carpenter bees most often resemble large bumblebees. They have black bodies with patches of yellow, and may be 1 inch long. Bees bore an individual tunnel approximately ¾ inch in diameter directly into wood, then turn at right angles and excavate extensive galleries running in the same direction as the wood grain in which they lay eggs. Control is the same as for carpenter ants.

Carpenter bee

INSECTS

Powder-post beetles

Beetle damage occurs chiefly in dry wood, including furniture. Adult beetles enter the wood through small natural openings, then lay eggs. The larvae then feed on the wood as they develop, causing damage that looks a great deal like termite damage. Beetles breed in the same wood generation upon generation, often for hundreds of years. Eventually the wood becomes so honeycombed with burrows that, as with termite damage, the structure collapses of its own weight. Evidence of beetle infestation is only slightly more noticeable from the outside than infestation by termites: Tiny "shot holes" in the wood where adult beetles have chewed their way to the outside—particularly during spring or early summer—as part of their life cycle.

In the U.S., three types of wood-boring beetles are collectively termed powder-post beetles. The two most common are the death watch beetle and the true powder-post beetle. Both are tiny—approximately ⅛ inch long. Death watches in America attack primarily Douglas fir (European species are known for destroying hardwoods), whereas powder-posts are attracted especially to hickory, ash, and oak. The third type, commonly called the lead cable borer, reaches 1 inch in length. Presently it thrives only in the semiarid southwest and California. Named for its habit of chewing into lead-lined electrical cables and similar articles during hot weather, this beetle is also prevalent in much furniture and paneling made of oak and California laurel wood.

As with termites, extermination by professionals is the only reliable control. Infested furniture can be removed from the home and fumigated in a special chamber; on-site extermination in such woodwork as paneling and floors requires residents to vacate the building for up to a few days.

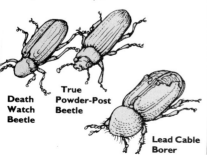

Death Watch Beetle **True Powder-Post Beetle** **Lead Cable Borer**

ERADICATING OTHER INSECT PESTS

CENTIPEDES AND MILLIPEDES

These multilegged pests inhabit damp, dark areas and decaying vegetable matter. Usually they remain out of doors; however, they may frequent unused basements and wander into the house from below or from outside. Some centipedes may bite if they are injured. If that happens, apply antiseptic to the swelling and call your physician if symptoms persist. To control centipedes and millipedes, apply insecticide on doorsills, windowsills, and other places where pests are entering the house. Pay particular attention to baseboard areas where pests may migrate from the basement.

EARWIGS

Easily recognized by their large rear pincers, these pests have become epidemic in many parts of the U.S. Earwigs inhabit moist, sheltered areas such as lawns and leafy garden vegetables, damp stored fabric or carpeting, the hollow tubing of lawn furniture, as well as foundation cracks, basements and behind baseboards. Control these pests with insecticide sprayed or applied to these areas. Major infestations are not a do-it-yourself proposition; seek professional pest-control advice.

CRICKETS

Crickets normally reside outdoors but may enter houses as autumn approaches or when populations increase during periodic cricket plagues. Whereas one or two of these insects are merely annoying because of their nocturnal chirping, an infestation can endanger many household items including woolens, silks and paper, not to mention fresh foodstuffs. To control crickets, spray insecticide around building entrances, baseboards and the edges of carpets. Also spray beneath furniture, in closets, and on floors behind drapery. Tight-fitting window screens and screen doors are effective along with other preventive measures to physically bar crickets from the house.

SPIDERS

Any area of undisturbed space within a house may be home to spiders; however, most prefer dark places. Though all spiders inject venom when they bite, only two species—the black widow and the brown recluse—are considered dangerous to humans. To be on the safe side, treat all spider bites with antiseptic and report them immediately to a physician. Regular and frequent sweeping and dusting can help keep spider populations down, but spraying insecticide is the best cure for infestations. To be sure of eradicating spiders, spray the webs with insecticide, then remove them after the spiders within them are dead. Black widows are especially fond of dry piles of lumber or firewood, and outdoor latrines. Use caution in these areas and spray often.

TICKS

Most ticks found in homes have been transported indoors by family pets, notably dogs. Filled with blood, the ticks drop off the animal and become lodged in bedding, upholstery, carpets and behind baseboards. Although many varieties of ticks carry diseases that affect humans, the common brown dog tick is considered harmless. To remove an individual tick, hold a lit cigarette close to its body, then pluck it away after it retracts its head from within the skin. You can also touch the tick with a red-hot needle, or swab it with kerosene or alcohol to remove it. Take an infested animal to a veterinarian for treatment. To effectively control ticks indoors, spray insecticide wherever an animal sleeps, and destroy old bedding by burning.

House Centipede

Millipede

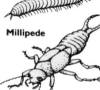

Earwig

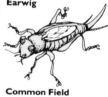

Common Field Cricket

Black Widow Spider

Brown Recluse Spider

Tick (engorged) and normal tick

INFESTATION: ANIMALS

SEE ALSO

◁ Details for:

| Insect infestation | 64–67 |

Domestic mouse
Not a serious threat to
health but they are
unhygienic.

Common rat
A serious health risk.
Seek expert advice.

Bat
Bats may cause rabies
and should be
considered a health
risk.

Rat damage to plug

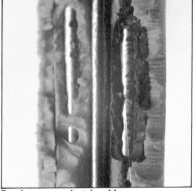

Rat damage to electric cable

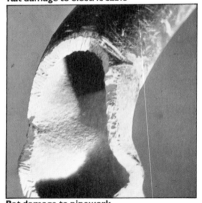

Rat damage to pipework

Insects aren't the only pests to set up home in your house: Mice and rats can be a menace, especially in houses that offer plenty of underfloor runs, where they can live and prosper uninterrupted and find a plentiful supply of food by invading your living quarters. Mice are a nuisance, but rats can be a definite health hazard and eradication is vital. Even bats are known to shelter inside houses, usually occupying the roof space, and although they're beneficial—consuming large quantities of insects—they also harbor rabies, a potentially fatal disease.

Mice

Mice will be attracted by fallen food scraps, so the best remedy is to keep the floors spotlessly clean. However, mice will move readily from house to house through the roof spaces and wall cavities and under floors, so it is sometimes difficult to eradicate them completely. Contact your local Health Department if the mice persist.

Poisoned bait can be obtained, which you should sprinkle onto a piece of paper or card. In this way, uneaten bait can be removed easily. Keep pets and children away from the bait. If signs of mice are still evident after three weeks, you should resort to a trap. Humane traps capture mice alive in a cage, so that you can deposit them elsewhere, or you can use the spring-loaded snap-traps.

Most people set too few traps. Ideally, place them every 6 feet across mouse runs. The best place is against the baseboard, facing the wall. Bait traps with flour, oatmeal or chocolate molded onto the bait hook. Dispose of the mouse bodies by burying, burning or flushing down the toilet.

Rats

Serious rat infestations rarely occur in the average domestic situation but they can be a problem in rural areas or near rivers and docks. They can be killed with anticoagulant poisons, but as rats are a health hazard, always contact the Health Department for expert advice.

Bats

Bats prefer to roost in uninhabited structures—farm buildings, caves, mines and tunnels—but occasionally they will inhabit domestic housing. If possible, bats should be left undisturbed, since they eat large numbers of insects—particularly flies and mosquitoes. Only a few species of tropical bats suck blood or do direct damage, such as eating fruit crops. However, bats are known to harbor diseases, particularly rabies, and as such, constitute a health hazard. To rid an attic of a bat colony, seal all the openings except one, and install a bright light to shine directly on the roosting area. Wait a week, then approximately ½ hour after dark (while any bats that haven't already left the premises are out feeding), seal the remaining opening. Should an individual bat stray into a room, try to keep calm. They will avoid you if possible—and they don't become entangled in hair as the old wives' tale suggests. Open all windows and doors to the outside, turn off the lights, and allow the bat to escape.

HANDLING POISONS SAFELY

Poisons designed to eradicate rodents are equally deadly to humans, so it is most important to follow the manufacturer's handling and storage instructions to the letter. Make sure poisons are always out of the reach of children, and where pets or other animals can get to them. Never store them under the kitchen sink where they might be mistaken for household products, or anywhere else where food could become contaminated. In the case of accidental consumption by animals or humans, keep the container so that the poison can be readily identified by a vet or doctor. Some containers are color-coded especially for the purpose. Wear protective gloves whenever you handle poisons and chemicals.

WET AND DRY ROT

Rot occurs in unprotected household timbers, fences and outbuildings, which are subjected to dampness. Fungal spores, which are always present, multiply and develop in these conditions until eventually the timber is destroyed. Fungal attack can be serious, requiring immediate attention to avoid very costly structural repairs to your home. There are two main scourges: wet and dry rot.

Recognizing rot

Signs of fungal attack are easy enough to detect but it is important to be able to identify certain strains which are much more damaging than others.

Mold growth
White, furry deposits or black spots on timber, plaster or wallpaper are mold growths; usually these are a result of condensation. When they are wiped or scraped from the surface, the structure shows no sign of physical deterioration apart from staining. Cure the source of the damp condition and treat the affected area with a solution of 16 parts warm water: 1 part bleach.

Wet rot

Wet rot occurs in timber with a high moisture content. As soon as the cause is eliminated, further deterioration is arrested. Wet rot frequently attacks the framework of doors and windows which have been neglected, enabling rainwater to penetrate joints or between brickwork and adjacent timbers. Peeling paintwork is often the first sign, which when removed reveals timber that is spongy when wet but dark brown and crumbly when dry. In advanced stages, the grain will have split and thin, dark brown fungal strands will be in evidence on the timber. Treat wet rot as soon as practicable.

Dry rot

Once it has taken hold, dry rot is a most serious form of decay. Urgent treatment is essential. It will attack timber with a much lower moisture content than wet rot, but—unlike wet rot, which thrives outdoors as well as indoors—only in poorly ventilated, confined spaces indoors.

Dry rot exhibits different characteristics depending on the extent of its development. It sends out fine, pale gray tubules in all directions, even through masonry, to seek out and infect other drier timber. It actually pumps water from damp timber and can progress at an alarming rate. The strands are accompanied by white cotton woollike growths, called mycelium, in very damp conditions. When established, dry rot develops wrinkled, pancake-shaped fruiting bodies, which produce rust-red spores that are expelled to rapidly cover surrounding timber and masonry. Infested timbers become brown and brittle, exhibiting cracks across and along the grain until it breaks up into little cubes. You may also detect a strong, musty, mushroomlike smell associated with the fungus.

Wet rot—treat it as early as possible

Dry rot—urgent treatment is essential

TREATING ROT

Dealing with wet rot
After eliminating the cause of the dampness, cut away and replace badly damaged wood, then paint the new and surrounding woodwork with three liberal applications of fungicidal wood preservative. Brush the liquid well into the joints and end grain.

Before decorating, you can apply a penetrating epoxy wood hardener to reinforce and rebuild damaged timbers, then repaint as normal.

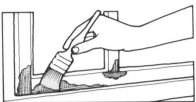

Fill rotted timbers with epoxy wood hardener

Dealing with dry rot
Dry rot requires more drastic action and should be treated by a specialist contractor, unless the outbreak is minor and self-contained. Remember that dry rot can penetrate masonry. Look under the floorboards in adjacent rooms before you are satisfied with the extent of the infection; check cavity walls for signs of rot.

Eliminate the source of water and ensure adequate ventilation in roof spaces or under the floors. Cut out all infected timber up to at least 1 foot 6 inches beyond the last visible sign of rot. Chop plaster from nearby walls, following the strands. Continue for another 1 foot 6 inches beyond the extent of the growth. Collect all debris in plastic bags and burn it or dispose of it away from the property.

Use a fungicidal preservative fluid to kill remaining spores. Wire-brush the masonry, then apply three liberal brush-coats to all timber, brickwork and plaster within 5 feet of the infected area. Alternatively, rent a sprayer and go over the same area three times.

If a wall was penetrated by strands of dry rot, drill regularly spaced but staggered holes into it from both sides. Angle the holes downwards so that fluid will collect in them to saturate the wall internally. Patch holes after treatment.

Treat replacement timbers and immerse the end grain in a bucket of fluid for five to ten minutes. If you are repairing a plaster eall, apply a zinc-oxychloride plaster.

SEE ALSO

Details for: ▷
Organic growth   24

ROT: PREVENTATIVE TREATMENT

Fungal attack can be so damaging that it is well worth taking precautions to prevent its occurrence. Regularly repaint and maintain window and door frames, where moisture can penetrate; seal around them with silicone caulk. Provide adequate ventilation between floors and ceilings; do the same in the attic. Check and eradicate any plumbing leaks and other sources of dampness, and you'll be less likely to experience the stranglehold rot can apply.

Looking after timberwork

Existing and new timbers can be treated with a preservative. Brush and spray three applications to standing timbers, paying particular attention to joints and end grain.

Immersing timbers

Timber in contact with the ground should be completely immersed in preservative. Stand fence posts on end in a bucket of fluid for 10 minutes. For other timbers, make a shallow bath from loose bricks and line it with thick polyethylene sheet. Pour preservative into the trough and immerse the timbers, weighing them down with bricks **(1)**. To empty the bath, sink a bucket at one end of the trough, then remove the bricks adjacent to it so the fluid pours out **(2)**, or use a bulb-type hand pump to suck up the liquid.

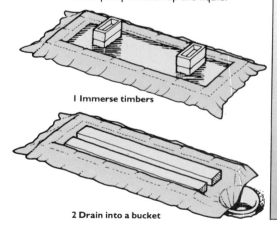

1 Immerse timbers

2 Drain into a bucket

WOOD PRESERVATIVES

Wood exposed to moisture should be treated with preservative to prevent rot. There are numerous types of wood preservatives, so be sure you choose the correct one for the timber you want to protect.

LIQUID PRESERVATIVES

For treatment of existing indoor and outdoor wood, choose a liquid preservative that you can apply by soaking or with a brush. Although all wood preservatives are toxic, the safest are copper and zinc napthenate, as well as copper-8-quinolinolate, tributyltin oxide (TBTO) and polyphase. Avoid using the traditional creosote or pentachlorophenol (penta). These chemicals are known carcinogens and highly toxic. If the wood must come into direct ground contact, use copper napthenate. Liquid preservatives, which are often sold as preservative stains, are readily available from paint stores, lumberyards and building supply stores.

PRESSURE-TREATED LUMBER

Consider using pressure-treated lumber for new outdoor construction and where wood will come in contact with ground or concrete. Use lumber stamped LP-22 for contact with soil; wood stamped LP-2 is only for above-ground use. Inhaling chemicals used to treat lumber can be harmful, so wear a mask when sawing and don't burn scraps.

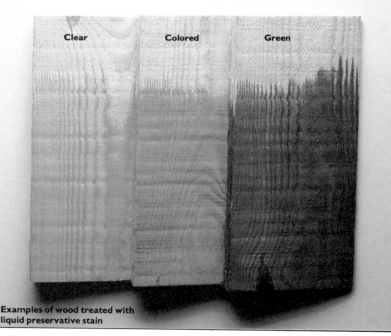

Clear   Colored   Green

Examples of wood treated with liquid preservative stain

SAFETY WITH PRESERVATIVES

All preservatives are flammable, so do not smoke while using them, and extinguish open flames.

    Wear protective gloves at all times when applying preservatives and wear a face mask when using these liquids indoors.

    Ensure good ventilation when the liquid is drying, and do not sleep in a freshly treated room for two nights to allow the fumes to dissipate fully.

REFERENCE & INDEX

BUILDING CODES, PERMITS AND OTHER LEGAL CONSIDERATIONS

OFFICIAL PERMISSION

Before starting certain building projects, it is necessary to obtain official permission from local authorities. Depending on the type of project and local regulations, you may need to apply for a building permit, zoning variance or a certificate of appropriateness. In some cases, you may need all three.

Building codes address nearly every detail of building construction from the acceptable recipes for concrete used in the foundation to the permissible fire rating of the roof finish material—and many features in between. Partly because codes attempt to be as comprehensive as possible and also because they must address different concerns in varied locales, they are very lengthy, complex and lack uniformity from region to region. A further complication is that many new building products become available each year that are not accounted for in existing codes. Model codes promulgated by four major organizations are widely used for reference throughout the United States.

The Uniform Building Code, published by the International Conference of Building Officials, is perhaps the most widely accepted code. ICBO republishes the entire code every three years and publishes revisions annually. A short form of the Uniform Building Code covering buildings with less than three stories and less than 6,000 square feet of ground floor area is available—easier for home builders, and remodelers' reference.

The BOCA-Basic Building Code, issued by the Building Officials and Code Administrators International, Inc., is also widely used. An abridged form designed for residential construction, which includes plumbing and wiring standards, is available.

A third model code, prepared under the supervision of the American Insurance Association and known as the National Building Code, serves as the basis for codes adopted by many communities. It, too, is available in a short form for matters related to home construction.

The Standard Building Code is published by the Southern Building Code Congress International, Inc. It addresses conditions and problems prevalent in the southern United States.

While it is likely that one of the model codes named above serves as the basis for the building code in your community, municipal governments and states frequently add standards and restrictions. It is your local building department that ultimately decides what is acceptable and what is not. Consult that agency if a code question should arise.

Building codes are primarily designed for the safety of the building occupants and the general welfare of the community at large. It is wise to follow *all* practices outlined by the prevailing code in your area.

Building permits

A building permit is generally required for new construction, remodeling projects that involve structural changes or additions, and major demolition projects. In some locales it may be necessary to obtain a building permit for constructing in-ground pools, and you may need a building permit or rigger's license to erect scaffolding as an adjunct to nonstructural work on a house.

To obtain a building permit, you must file forms prescribed by your local building department that answer questions about the proposed site and project. In addition, it is necessary to file a complete set of drawings of the project along with detailed specifications. A complete set normally includes a plot plan or survey, foundation plan, floor plans, wall sections and electrical, plumbing and mechanical plans. Building permit fees are usually assessed based on the estimated cost of construction and records of the application are usually passed along to the local tax department for reassessment of the property value.

At the time you apply for a building permit, you may be advised of other applications for official permission that are required. For example, you may need to apply to the county health department concerning projects that may affect sewerage facilities and natural water supplies. It is important to arrange inspections in a timely way since finish stages cannot proceed until the structural, electrical, plumbing and mechanical work are approved.

Anyone may apply for a building permit, but it is usually best to have an architect or contractor file in your behalf, even if you plan to do the work yourself.

Zoning restrictions

Even for projects that do not require a building permit, local zoning regulations may limit the scope and nature of the construction permitted. Whereas building codes and permit regulations relate to a building itself, zoning rules address the needs and conditions of the community as a whole by regulating the development and uses of property. Zoning restrictions may apply to such various cases as whether a single-family house can be remodeled into apartments, whether a commercial space can be converted to residential use or the permissible height of a house or outbuilding.

It is advisable to apply to the local zoning board for approval before undertaking any kind of construction or remodeling that involves a house exterior or yard or if the project will substantially change the way a property is used. If the project does not conform with the standing zoning guidelines, you may apply to the zoning board for a variance. It is best to enlist the help of an architect or attorney for this.

Landmark regulations

Homes in historic districts may be subject to restrictions placed to help the neighborhood retain its architectural distinction and character. For the most part in designated landmark areas, changes in house exteriors are closely regulated. While extensive remodeling that would significantly change the architectural style are almost never permitted, even seemingly small modifications of existing structures are scrutinized. For example, metal or vinyl replacement windows may not be permitted for Victorian homes in designated areas, or the exterior paint and roof colors may be subject to approval. Even the color of the mortar used to repoint brickwork may be specified by the local landmarks commission or similar regulating body. Designs for new construction must conform to the prevalent architectural character. If you live in an historic district, it is advised that you apply to the governing body for approval of any plans for exterior renovation.

WILL YOU NEED A PERMIT OR VARIANCE?

Building code requirements and zoning regulations vary from city to city and frequently have county and state restrictions added to them. For this reason, it is not possible to state categorically which

home-improvement projects require official permission and which do not. The chart below, which lists some of the most frequently undertaken projects, is meant to serve as a rough guide. Taken as a whole,

it suggests a certain logic for anticipating when and what type of approval may be needed. Whether or not official approval is required, all work should be carried out in conformity with local code standards.

TYPE OF WORK	BUILDING PERMIT NEEDED		ZONING APPROVAL NEEDED	
Exterior painting and repairs / Interior decoration and repairs	NO	Permit or rigger's license may be needed to erect exterior scaffolding	NO	Certificate of appropriateness may be needed in historic areas
Replacing windows and doors	NO		NO	Permissible styles may be restricted in historic districts
Electrical	NO	Have work performed or checked by a licensed contractor	NO	Outdoor lighting may be subject to approval
Plumbing	NO	Have work performed or checked by a licensed contractor	NO	Work involving new water supply, septic or sewerage systems may require county health department
Heating	NO		NO	Installation of new oil storage tanks may require state environmental agency approval
Constructing patios and decks	Possibly		Possibly	
Installing a hot tub	NO		NO	
Structural alterations	YES		NO	Unless alterations change building height above limit or proximity of building to lot line
Attic remodeling	NO	Ascertain whether joists can safely support the floor load	NO	
Building a fence or garden wall	NO		YES	In cases where structure is adjacent to public road or easement or extends above a height set by board
Planting a hedge	NO		NO	
Path or sidewalk paving	NO		Possibly	Public sidewalks must conform to local standards and specifications
Clearing land	NO		YES	County and state environmental approval may also be needed
Constructing an in-ground pool	YES		YES	County and state environmental approval may also be needed
Constructing outbuildings	YES	For buildings larger than set limit	Possibly	
Adding a porch	NO	Unless larger than set limit	Possibly	Regulations often set permissible setback from public road
Adding a sunspace or greenhouse	YES		Possibly	Yes, if local rules apply to extensions
Constructing a garage	YES		Possibly	Yes, if used for a commercial vehicle and within set proximity to lot line
Driveway paving	NO		Possibly	Yes where access to public road created, also restrictions on proximity to lot lines
Constructing a house extension	YES		Possibly	Regulations may limit permissible house size and proximity to lot lines
Demolition	YES	If work involves structural elements	NO	Structures in historic districts may be protected by regulations
Converting 1-family house to multiunit dwelling	YES	Fire safety and ventilation codes are frequently more stringent for multiple dwellings	YES	
Converting a residential building to commercial use	YES		YES	

If you have a question about whether you need to file for a building permit or obtain a zoning variance, consult with your local building department.

BUILDER'S TOOL KIT

Bricklayers, carpenters and plasterers are all specialist builders, each requiring a set of specific tools, but the amateur is more like one of the self-employed builders who must be able to tackle several areas of building work, and so need a much wider range of tools than the specialist. The builder's tool kit suggested here is for renovating and improving the structure of a house and for erecting and restoring garden structures or paving. Electrical work, decorating and plumbing call for other sets of tools.

FLOATS AND TROWELS

For professional builders, floats and trowels have specific uses, but in home maintenance, the small towel for repointing brickwork is often found ideal for patching small areas of plaster, while the plasterer's trowel is as likely to be used for smoothing concrete.

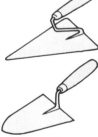

Using a pointing tray
A pointing try makes the filling of mortar joints very easy. Place the flat lip of the tray just under a horizontal joint and scrape the mortar into place with a jointer. Turn the tray around and push mortar into vertical joints through the gap between the raised sides.

Continental-pattern trowels

● **Essential tools**
Brick trowel
Pointing trowel
Plasterer's trowel
Mortar board
Hawk
Level
Try square
Plumb line

74

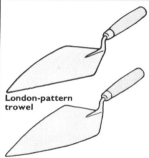

London-pattern trowel

Canadian-pattern trowel
Brick trowel
A brick trowel is for handling and placing mortar when laying bricks or concrete blocks. A professional might use one with a blade as long as 1 foot, but such a trowel is too heavy and unwieldy for the amateur, so buy a good-quality brick trowel with a fairly short blade.

The blade of a **London-pattern trowel** has one curved edge for cutting bricks, a skill that needs much practice to perfect. The blade's other edge is straight, for picking up mortar. This type of trowel is made in right- and left-handed versions, so buy the right one. A right-handed trowel has its curved edge on the right when you point it away from you.

A **Canadian-pattern trowel** is symmetrical, so it's convenient when people with different left- and right-hand preferences have to share one trowel.

Pointing trowel
The blade of a pointing trowel is no more than 3 to 4 inches long, designed for repairing or shaping mortar joints between bricks.

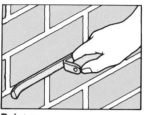

Pointer
A pointer is shaped for making 'V' or concave joints between bricks. The narrow blade is dragged along the mortar joint and the curved front end is used to shape the verticals.

Frenchman
A Frenchman is a specialized tool for cutting excess mortar away from brickwork jointing. You can make one by heating and bending an old table knife.

Wooden float
A wooden float is for applying and smoothing stucco and concrete to a fine, attractive texture. The more expensive ones have detachable handles so that their wooden blades can be replaced when they wear. But the amateur is unlikely to use a float often enough to justify the cost of buying one.

Plasterer's trowel
A plasterer's trowel is a steel float for applying plaster and stucco to walls. It is also dampened and used for "polishing," stroking the surface of the material when it has firmed up. Some builders prefer to apply stucco with a heavy trowel and finish it with a more flexible blade, but one has to be quite skilled to exploit such subtle differences.

BOARDS FOR CARRYING MORTAR OR PLASTER

Any convenient-sized sheet of ½- or ¾-inch exterior-grade plywood can be used as a mixing board for plaster or mortar. A panel about 3 feet square is ideal, and a smaller spotboard, about 2 feet square, is convenient for carrying the material to the actual work site. In either case, screw some wood strips to the undersides of the boards to make them easier to lift and carry. Make a small, lightweight hawk to carry pointing mortar or plaster by nailing a single strip underneath a plywood board so that you can plug a handle into it.

A homemade hawk

LEVELING AND MEASURING TOOLS

You can make several specialized tools for measuring and leveling, but don't skimp on essentials like a good level and a strong tape measure.

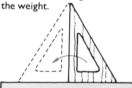

Level
A level is a machine-made straightedge incorporating special glass tubes or vials that contain a liquid. In each vial an air bubble floats. When a bubble rests exactly between two lines marked on the glass, the structure on which the level is held is known to be exactly horizontal or vertical, depending on the vial's orientation. Buy a wooden or lightweight aluminum level 2 to 3 feet long. A well-made one is very strong, but treat it with care and always clean mortar or plaster from it before the material sets.

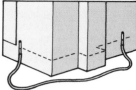

Water level
You can make a water level from a garden hose with short lengths of transparent plastic tube plugged into its ends. Fill the hose with water until it appears in both tubes. As water level is constant, the levels in the tubes are always identical and so can be used for marking identical heights even over long distances and around obstacles and bends.

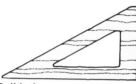

Builder's square
A large set square is useful when you set out brick or concrete-block corners. The best ones are stamped out of sheet metal, but you can make a serviceable one by cutting out a thick plywood right-angled triangle with a hypotenuse of about 2 feet 6 inches. Cut out the center of the triangle to reduce the weight.

Checking a square
Accuracy is important, so check the square by placing it against a straight strip of wood on the floor, drawing a line against the square to make a right angle with the strip, then turning the square to see if it forms the same angle from the other side.

Try square
Use a try square for marking out square cuts or joints on timber.

Making a plumb line
Any small but heavy weight hung on a length of line or string will make a suitable plumb line for judging the verticality of structures or surfaces.

Bricklayer's line

Use a bricklayer's line as a guide for laying bricks or blocks level. It is a length of nylon string stretched between two flat-bladed pins that are driven into vertical joints at the ends of a wall. There are also special line blocks that hook over the bricks at the ends of a course. As an improvisation, you can stretch a string between two stakes driven into the ground outside the line of the wall.

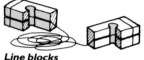

Steel pins and line
Buy the special pins or make your own by hammering flats on 4-inch nails.

Line blocks
Blocks grip the brickwork corners; the line passes through their slots.

Plasterer's rule
A plasterer's rule is simply a straight wooden strip used for scraping plaster and rendering undercoats level.

Straightedge
Any length of straight, fairly stout lumber can be used to tell whether a surface is flat or, used with a level, to test whether two points are at the same height.

Gauge stick
For gauging the height of brick courses, calibrate a wooden strip by making saw cuts across it at 3-inch intervals—the thickness of a brick plus its mortar joint.

Tape measure
An ordinary retractable steel tape measure is adequate for most purposes, but if you need to mark out or measure a large plot, rent a wind-up tape up to 100 feet in length.

Marking gauge
This tool has a sharp steel point for scoring a line on lumber parallel to its edge. Its adjustable stock acts as a fence and keeps the point a constant distance from the edge.

HAMMERS

Very few hammers are needed on a building site.

Claw hammer
Choose a strong claw hammer for building wooden stud partitions, nailing floorboards, making door and window frames and putting up fencing.

Light sledgehammer
A light sledgehammer is used for driving cold chisels and for various demolition jobs. It is also useful for driving large masonry nails into walls.

Sledgehammer
Rent a big sledgehammer if you have to break up concrete or paving. It's also the best tool for driving stakes or fence posts into the ground, though you can make do with a light sledge if the ground is not too hard.

Mallet
A carpenter's wooden mallet is the proper tool for driving wood chisels, but you can use a hammer if the chisels have impact-resistant plastic handles.

SAWS

Every builder needs a range of handsaws, but consider renting a power saw when you have to cut a lot of heavy structural timbers, and especially if you plan to rip floorboards down to width, a very tiring job when done by hand.

There are special power saws for cutting metal, and even for sawing through masonry.

Panel saw
All kinds of man-made building boards are used in house construction, so buy a good panel saw—useful also for cutting large structural timbers to the required lengths.

Tenon saw
A tenon saw accurately cuts wall studs, floorboards, panelling and joints. The metal stiffening along the top of the blade keeps it rigid and less likely to wander off line.

Padsaw
Also called a keyhole saw, this small saw has a narrow tapered blade for cutting holes in wood.

Coping saw
A coping saw has a frame that holds a fairly coarse but very narrow blade under tension for cutting curves in wood.

Floorboard saw
If you pry a floorboard above its neighbors you can cut across it with an ordinary tenon saw. But a floorboard saw's curved cutting edge makes it easier to avoid damaging the boards on either side.

Hacksaw
The hardened-steel blades of a hacksaw have fine teeth for cutting metal. Use one to cut steel concrete-reinforcing rods or small pieces of sheet metal.

Sheet saw
A hacksaw's frame prevents its use for cutting large sheets of metal. For that job, bolt a hacksaw blade to the edge of the flat blade of a sheet saw, which will also cut corrugated plastic sheeting and roofing slates.

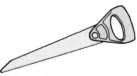

Universal saw
A universal or general-purpose saw is designed to cut wood, metal, plastics and building boards. Its short frameless blade has a low-friction coating and is stiff enough to make straight cuts without wandering. The handle can be set at various angles. The saw is particularly useful for cutting secondhand lumber, which may contain nails or screws that would blunt an ordinary saw.

POWER SAWS

A *circular saw* will accurately rip lumber or man-made boards down to size. As well as doing away with the effort of hand-sawing large timbers, a sharp power saw produces such a clean cut that there is often no need for planing afterwards.

A *power jigsaw* cuts curves in lumber and sheet materials but is also useful for cutting holes in fixed wall panels and sawing through floorboards so as to lift them.

A *reciprocating saw* is a two-handed power saw with a long pointed blade, powerful enough to cut heavy timber sections and even through a complete stud partition, panels and all.

Masonry saw
A masonry saw looks much like a wood handsaw but its tungsten-carbide teeth cut brick, concrete blocks and stone.

DRILLS

A powerful electric drill is invaluable to a builder, but a hand brace is useful when you have to bore holes outdoors or in attics and cellars that lack convenient electric sockets.

Power drill
Buy a power drill, a range of twist drills and some spade or power-bore bits for drilling lumber. Make sure that the tool has a percussion or hammer action for drilling masonry. For masonry you need special drill bits tipped with tungsten carbide. The smaller ones are matched to the size of standard wall plugs, though there are much larger ones with reduced shanks that can be used in a standard power-drill chuck. The larger bits are expensive, so rent them when you need them. Percussion bits are even tougher than masonry bits, with shatterproof tips.

Brace and bit
A brace and bit is the ideal hand tool for drilling large holes in lumber, and when fitted with a screwdriver bit, it gives good leverage for driving or extracting large woodscrews.

Drilling masonry for wall plugs
Set the drill for low speed and hammer action, and wrap tape around the bit to mark the depth to be drilled. Allow for slightly more depth than the length of the plug, as dust will pack down into the hole when you insert it. Drill the hole in stages.

Protect floor coverings and paintwork from falling dust by taping a paper bag under the position of the hole before you start drilling.

● **Essential tools**
Straightedge
Tape measure
Claw hammer
Light sledgehammer
Panel saw
Tenon saw
Hacksaw
Padsaw
Power drill
Masonry bits
Brace and bit

ADDITIONAL BUILDER'S TOOLS

The following tools would be a useful addition to a builder's tool kit, especially when carrying out major repairs and improvements.

Crowbar

A crowbar, or wrecking bar, is for demolishing timber framework. Force the flat tip between components and use the leverage of the long shaft to pry them apart. Choose a bar that has a claw at one end for removing large nails.

• **Essential tools**
Glass cutter
Putty knife
Cold chisel
Bricklayer's chisel
Spade
Shovel
Rake
Wheelbarrow
Cabinet screwdriver
Phillips-head screwdriver
Jack plane

GLAZIER'S TOOLS

Glass is such a hard and brittle material that it can be worked only with specialized tools.

Glass cutter

A glass cutter doesn't really cut glass but scores a line in it. The scoring is done by a tiny hardened-steel wheel or a chip of industrial diamond mounted in the penlike holder. The glass will break along the scored line when pressure is applied to it.

Beam compass cutter

A beam compass cutter is for scoring circles on glass—when, for example, you need a round hole in a window pane to fit a ventilator. The cutting wheel is mounted at the end of an adjustable beam that turns on a center pivot which is fixed to the glass by suction.

Spear-point glass drill

A glass drill has a flat spearhead-shaped tip of tungsten-steel shaft. The shape of the tip reduces friction that would otherwise crack the glass, but it needs lubricating with oil, paraffin or water during drilling.

Hacking knife

A hacking knife has a heavy steel blade for chipping old putty out of window rabbets so as to remove the glass. Place its point between the putty and the frame and tap its thickened back with a hammer.

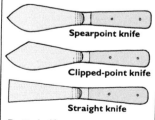

Spearpoint knife

Clipped-point knife

Straight knife

Putty knife

The blunt blade of a putty knife is for shaping and smoothing fresh putty. You can choose between spearpoint, clipped-point and straight blades according to your personal preference.

CHISELS

As well as chisels for cutting and paring wood joints, you will need some special ones for masonry work.

Cold chisel

Cold chisels are made from solid steel hexagonal-section rod. They are primarily for cutting metal bars and chopping the heads off rivets, but a builder will use one for cutting a chase in plaster and brickwork or chopping out old brick pointing.

Slip a plastic safety sleeve over the chisel to protect your hand from a misplaced blow with the sledgehammer.

Plugging chisel

A plugging chisel has a flat narrow bit (tip) for cutting out old pointing. It's worth renting one if you have a large area of brickwork to repoint.

Bricklayer's chisel

The wide bit of a bricklayer's chisel is for cutting bricks and concrete blocks. It's also useful for levering up floorboards.

WORK GLOVES

Wear strong work gloves whenever you carry paving stones, concrete blocks or rough lumber. Ordinary gardening gloves are better than none but won't last long on a building site. The best work gloves have leather palms and fingers, though you may prefer a pair with ventilated backs for comfort in hot weather.

DIGGING TOOLS

Much building work requires some kind of digging—for laying strip foundations and concrete pads, sinking rows of postholes and so on. You may already have the essential tools in your garden shed; others you can rent.

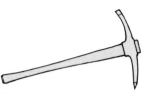

Pickaxe

Use a medium-weight pickaxe to break up heavily compacted soil, especially if it contains a lot of buried rubble.

Mattlock

The wide blade of a mattock is ideal for breaking up heavy clay soil, and it's better than an ordinary pickaxe for ground that's riddled with tree roots.

Spade

Buy a good-quality spade for excavating soil and mixing concrete. One with a stainless-steel blade is best, but alloy steel will last fairly well if it is looked after. For strength choose a D-shaped handle whose hardwood shaft has been split and riveted with metal plates to the crosspiece, and make sure that the shaft socket and blade are forged in one piece.

Square blades seem to be the most popular, though some builders prefer a round-mouth spade with a long pole handle for digging deep trenches and holes.

Shovel

You can use a spade for mixing and placing concrete or mortar, but the raised edges of a shovel retain it better.

Garden rake

Use an ordinary garden rake to spread gravel or level wet concrete, but be sure to wash it before any concrete sets on it.

Posthole auger

Rent a posthole auger to sink narrow holes for fence and gate posts by driving it into the ground like a corkscrew and pulling out plugs of earth.

Wheelbarrow

The average garden wheelbarrow is not really strong enough for work on building sites, which entails carrying heavy loads of wet concrete and rubble. Unless the tubular underframe is rigidly strutted, the barrow's thin metal body will distort and perhaps spill its load as you cross rough ground. Check, too, that the axle is fixed securely. Cheap wheelbarrows often lose their wheels when their loads are being tipped into excavations.

SCREWDRIVERS

One's choice of screwdrivers is a personal matter, and most people accumulate a collection of types and sizes over the years.

Cabinet screwdriver

Buy at least one large flat-tip screwdriver. The fixed variety is quite adequate but a pump-action one, which drives large screws very quickly, is useful when you assemble big wooden building structures.

Phillips-head screwdriver

Choose the size and type of Phillips-head screwdriver to suit the work at hand. There is no most useful size as the driver must fit the screw slots exactly.

PLANES

Your choice of planes depends on the kind of joinery you plan to do. Sophisticated framing may call for molding or grooving planes, but most woodwork needs only skimming to leave a fairly smooth finish.

Jack plane

A medium-size bench plane, the jack plane, is the best general-purpose tool.

GLOSSARY OF TERMS

Aggregate
Particles of sand or stone mixed with cement and water to make concrete, or added to paint to make a textured finish.

Alkali-resistant primer
A primer used to prevent the alkali content of some building materials from attacking a subsequent coat of oil-based paint.

Batter
The slope of the face of a wall that leans backward or tapers from bottom to top.

Blown
To have broken away, as when a layer of cement stucco has parted from a wall.

Bond
The staggered pattern of bricks designed to spread the static load along a wall and to tie the individual units together.

Boundary wall
A wall that defines the line or furthest limit of an area of property.

Capping strip
A length of wood nailed to the top edge of a fence panel.

Cavity wall
A wall of two separate masonry skins with an air space between them.

Control joint
A continuous joint built into a wall or concrete base to allow for expansion.

Coping
The top course of bricks or slabs of a wall, designed to shed rainwater to prevent moisture from seeping into the upper joints of the masonry.

Counterbore
To cut a hole that allows the head of a bolt or screw to lie below a surface. *or* The hole itself.

Damp-proof course
A layer of impervious material which prevents moisture from rising from the ground into the walls of a building.

Damp-proof membrane
A layer of impervious material which prevents moisture from rising through a concrete floor; vapor barrier.

Datum point
The point from which measurements are taken.

Door framing
The lining of wood used to finish the inner edges of a masonry door opening.

DPC
See *damp-proof course.*

DPM
See *damp-proof membrane.*

Drip groove
A groove cut or molded in the underside of a door or windowsill to prevent rainwater from running back to the wall.

Efflorescence
A white powdery deposit caused by soluble salts migrating to the surface of masonry.

Featherboarding
Strips of wood with a tapered section, used as components for a closeboard fence.

Footing
A narrow concrete foundation for a wall.

Frass
Powdered wood produced by the activity of woodworm.

Hardcore
Broken bricks or stones used to form a subbase below foundations, paving, etc.

Heave
An upward swelling of the ground caused by excess moisture.

Hoggin
A fine ballast, usually with a clay content, used to form a subbase for concrete pads or paving.

Insulation
Materials used to reduce the transmission of heat or sound.

Jamb
The vertical side member of a door or window frame; sometimes the frame as a whole.

Lead
A stepped section of brick- or blockwork built at each end of a wall to act as a guide to the height of the intermediate coursing.

Lintel
A horizontal beam used to support the wall over a door or window opening.

Marine plywood
Plywood meeting specific APA requirements governing continuing immersion in fresh and salt water.

Mastic
A nonsetting compound used to seal joints.

Masonry bolt
A fixing device designed to anchor itself in a masonry wall by expansion.

Microporous
Used to describe a finish that allows wood to dry out while protecting it from rainwater.

Piers
Columns of brick- or blockwork used to buttress a wall at regular intervals or to form a gateway.

Prefabricate
To manufacture components in a factory or workshop, which are then easily transported to and erected on site.

Primer
The first coat of a paint system to protect the workpiece and reduce absorption of subsequent coats.

Retaining wall
A wall built against a bank of earth to prevent it from slipping.

Scratchcoat
The bottom layer of cement stucco.

Set
A small rectangular paving block.

Shim
A thin packing strip.

Soakaway
A pit filled with rubble or gravel into which water is drained.

Spalling
Flaking of the outer face of masonry caused by expanding moisture in icy conditions.

Stucco
A thin layer of cement-based mortar applied to exterior walls to provide a protective finish. Sometimes fine stone aggregate is embedded in the mortar. *or* To apply the mortar.

Stud partition
An interior stud-framed dividing wall.

Studs
The vertical members of a stud-framed wall.

Subsidence
A sinking of the ground casued by the shrinkage of excessively dry soil.

Tamp
To pack down firmly with repeated blows.

Thixotropic
A property of some paints which have a jellylike consistency until stirred or applied, at which point they become liquefied.

Weep hole
A small hole at the base of a cavity wall to allow absorbed water to drain to the outside.